Michelle

Carolyn E. Phillips

Regal Books

A Division of G L Publications
Ventura. CA. U.S.A.

The foreign language publishing of all Regal books is under the direction of GLINT. GLINT provides financial and technical help for the adaptation, translation and publishing of books in more than 85 languages for millions of people worldwide.

For more information write: GLINT, P.O. Box 6688, Ventura, California 93006.

Published by Regal Books
A Division of G/L Publications
Ventura, California 93006
Printed in U.S.A.

Library of Congress Catalog Card No. 80-52202
ISBN 0-8307-0757-3

Code Number: 5109000

Contents

Dedication

This book is
lovingly dedicated
to the memory of

Sheli Lois Hansen
October 13, 1974 to
September 26,1979
Her contagious enjoyment
of all God's creations and
unwaivering acceptance of life
as it unfolded
make her short five years
an unquenchable inspiration
to those of us who love her
so very, very much.
Time will never
take her from us.

Preface

When I told Wayne Newton I was writing a book about Michelle Price he raised his eyebrows and said slowly, "You've undertaken a monumental task." Nearly a year later the book is complete and I've learned that *monumental* was an understatement. Trying to capture Michelle's spark and enthusiasm has been an incredible challenge, the sweetest challenge of my writing career thus far.

At twelve years old, Michelle can be found walking gracefully down a flight of stairs or zipping down the banister. She can talk your arm off or sit quietly, an attentive listener. But she is always ready to love you.

Love overflows the Price household and those who know them know their love. Dick and Laura have an ability to gently draw others out, without revealing their own hardships. Many people they meet have no idea of the magnitude of trials this family has shared. Dick and Laura are busy loving others, supporting someone who may be hurting.

The story you are about to read is one of love in growth. Friends and professionals, communities and clergy were sacrificially supportive to the Prices in their times of need. Much has been left unsaid because no book could contain it all. Some of the characters you'll meet are combinations of several people, patched together to give the story a readable flow. But this is the true story of Michelle—the portrait of a victor.

Author's Acknowledgments

Thanks to the many people whose cooperation and support have made this book possible.

First and foremost my heartfelt thanks to Michelle and her delightful family—now, treasured friends. You opened your hearts and hurts to me, pushing back into painful memories to share your story. Your active, day-by-day faith walk has been an example to me over and over again.

To my husband, Chip, and our children, Rob and Cara, for your countless silent trips past my closed door. I couldn't have done it without you.

To my parents for the setting—a writer's dream—for more than your fair share of moral support, and for all the free food.

To Robert VanKampen for your personal endorsement of the manuscript.

To Terri Hansen for tons of typing.

To Linda Kurz for introducing me to the Prices and for the finest friendship on wheels.

To the many people who were so generous with their time and observations about Michelle and her family, especially Dr. Robert Rosen of the City of Hope and Mr. Wayne Newton.

Special thanks to my dear friend Cheri Hansen whose sensitive reading and rereading of the manuscript inspired compassion and empathy in this writer's heart. For the pain it caused you, Cheri, my continued respect and gratitude.

And to our miraculous Lord for the marvelous way He weaves the tapestries of our lives together for His perfect purpose.

The Family's Acknowledgments

We want to publicly thank our older daughter, Kim, for the supportive part she played in helping care for Rick and Michelle. She selflessly carried more than her share of the load, hurting deeply with us, encouraging us when we needed it and giving of herself with no concern for the cost. Thank you, Kim, for being you. We're crazy about you!

We both want to thank our parents for the consistent Christian example their lives have always been to us. We are very proud to be a part of a fine Christian heritage. Our gratitude encompasses *every member* of the family. You've *each* added so much to our lives.

To modern "medicine men and women" who trust their knowledge *and* their hearts. Dr. Glick, we'll never be able to thank you enough for suspecting more than medicine could prove and following your feelings that November morning.

To Riverside Thrift and Loan a special thanks for reasons only you will fully understand.

To NHSRA, Winter Park and Hal O'Leary our warmest thanks and deepest gratitude for opening a new world to Michelle.

To the City of Hope, the Sportsmen's Club and Bill Hughes for caring so deeply, for giving from the heart.

To Wayne for giving of yourself, for being a friend, for loving our daughter.

To Dellene for helping make a dream come true.

There are many other people who have become a part of our lives and have given so much to us—*prayer*, love and support. It would be virtually impossible to name names here. Experiencing the outpouring of love so sincerely and warmly expressed has sustained us in difficult times and demonstrated our Lord's command to love one another. The only way we'll ever be able to thank you for *your* love is to reach out to others as you have to us.

We must express our appreciation to Carolyn Phillips for the many hours of effort, joy and tears that you have expended in reliving our story with us. In writing this book you have cried when we cried, laughed when we laughed and caught the spirit of our lives on paper. Even more important to us are the prayers you offered in our behalf—before we'd met, before there was "a book."

1
Needing a Miracle

"Death has to be waiting at the end of the ride before you truly see the earth, and feel your heart, and love the world."
—Jean Anouilh, *The Lark*

Dr. Abrams's stylish wooden heels clicked on the brown tile floor as she walked briskly into the crowded waiting room. "I've seen the biopsy reports on Michelle," she said, singling out a man and woman sitting stiffly upright on a chrome-legged couch.

Dick Price pulled himself up to his full six-foot two-inch height and looked down at the small-framed woman in charge of his daughter's case here at Children's Hospital.

Dr. Abrams slipped her hands into the starched white pockets of her lab coat and said, "She's got bone cancer. We'll have to take the leg right away."

Dick gulped in air, struggling to get a deep breath. He felt as if he'd been hit in the stomach as he sank back onto the couch. His dazed mind was buzzing, trying to comprehend what he'd just heard, "Michelle has cancer."

Laura sat motionless beside her husband Dick, stunned and silent. Her heart pounded in her ears and time ground to a halt around her. She felt like an observer, watching a play unfolding one scene at a time.

She shut her eyes against the words Doctor Abrams spoke, then forced them open again, afraid of the darkness that enveloped her. "You can't mean that," she said shaking her head, denying the cancer. "You can't take her leg. She's only eight years old!" Her voice sounded strange to her, as if it came from someone else. Tears blurred her vision as she searched the doctor's face for a glimmer of hope she knew was not there.

In the chair beside her, Michelle's 17-year-old sister, Kim, buried her head in both hands and cried deep, soul-wracking sobs. Laura reached out touching Kim's arm. She felt sick and empty, helpless to comfort her daughter.

"What she's got," the doctor continued in a clinical tone of voice, "is *osteogenic sarcoma,* a very fast, very deadly kind of bone cancer. You have to understand, her chances of beating this are extremely slim, less than four percent."

"You mean, only four in a hundred live with—?"

She interrupted Dick, "*Less* than four in a hundred, actually. I want you to be realistic about this from the beginning. The type of cancer your daughter has is extremely difficult to deal with."

People sitting around the waiting room grew uneasy. Some idly turned pages in tattered magazines. Others nervously glanced toward Dick and Laura, then quickly looked away again, embarrassed—like children peeking at forbidden things, afraid of being caught in the act.

"I'm going up to talk to Michelle," the doctor reported, moving quickly into the hallway. "I'll let you know about the surgery time—"

"Wait a minute," Dick said, springing to his feet and following her from the room, "we're not sure that's what we're going to do yet."

"There's no time to waste!" She replied, agitated. *He's too concerned, too cautious and only a layman. There isn't time for that now,* she thought to herself.

"There's no room for a mistake in something like this either." Dick answered looking directly into her eyes. He could feel her resistance but he was standing his ground. "We want another opinion."

"That's up to you," she said curtly, her expression cold. "Let me know."

Turning smartly on her heel she walked away without looking back.

They stood staring blankly after her, lost in their thoughts, unaware of clacking typewriters and the nasal buzzing of the busy hospital switchboard just beyond them in the lobby. Submerged in helplessness and fear, they watched as Dr. Abrams disappeared around the corner.

Dick suddenly felt much older than his 40 some years. The pain and tension of the past few days were taking their toll much too fast; he looked older, worn and tired.

Laura, her face suddenly pale, reached for Dick's hand. A week ago their lives had been so normal. Kim was involved in senior pep squad finals; Rick, the oldest, was working hard at his new job at the gas station. And Michelle was adjusting well to the routine of a third grader.

When Michelle complained about her right leg hurting, Laura thought it seemed a little swollen and warm to the touch. But she was sure it was nothing serious. She called the family doctor expecting the problem to be shin splints or a need for corrective shoes at most. But something in the doctor's "I don't like it," made her blood run cold. Even at that she never dreamed it might be this bad—*never*—cancer!

Dr. Abrams is a good doctor, a specialist, Laura thought as she struggled to stay composed. *Our doctor recommended her so highly.* She quickly reviewed the past few days. *Everything's happened so fast! A biopsy two days ago and now—now she says Michelle's going to lose her leg? A bad dream, that's what it is, a nightmare!* Fear and frustration mounted. She walked a few steps away from Dick. What she wanted to do was run as far and as fast as she could. Yet she knew she had to stay.

Kim leaned against the thick plaster wall outside the waiting room. "How can she be so hard?" she asked angrily. Her voice cracked as tears pressed against her throat. "How could *anybody* do what she just did?" Like a sudden summer shower, tears ran down her face.

Laura walked quickly to Kim's side and put both arms around the trembling girl. "I guess she's just doing her job, honey," she said not really convinced herself.

"Then why do I feel like she hit me?" Kim cried. "That woman's like a tank!"

"I don't like her methods either," Dick spoke hotly, "but we can't change her. What we can do is find someone else to work with."

"Do you think she might be right?" Laura asked. She reached for Dick's arm, suddenly very weak.

"I don't know what to think," he pondered running his fingers through his slightly graying hair. "I'm sure she's a good doctor. Everyone we've talked to seems to think so highly of her. And we *know* it's a good hospital." Thoughtfully he reviewed the facts and weighed his anxieties—he didn't feel confident in Dr. Abrams. "I still think we need to talk to somebody else," he said, the decision made.

"I wouldn't want her operating on me," Kim added, her eyes flashing anger. Usually good-natured, Kim was fiercely protective of her family, especially Michelle.

The three of them walked toward the elevator. As Laura reached out to press the button, Dick caught her hand and pulled her into his arms, then reached around Kim and drew her close to them both. They stood holding tightly to each other, tears washing over the pain that pierced them so deeply.

"Oh, Dick," Laura cried as she clung to him, "I'd give anything if it could be me instead!"

"I know," he comforted, straining for control as tears flowed down his face. "We'd all trade if we could."

"Why Shelly, Daddy?" Kim asked. "Why?"

"Oh, God!" Dick sobbed holding his family close to him, "We need you now like we've never needed you before. Please, make us strong—"

He whispered hoarsely, "Somehow God's going to get us through this."

They struggled for composure as they walked back to the elevator, then waited while a group stepped off. Three women talking in low voices walked toward the door. Behind them followed a teenage girl. Her eyes were red-rimmed and she tightly clutched a stuffed turtle. An older couple, arm in arm, completed the group.

Laura found herself wondering whether these people were there to see children as ill as Michelle. Her heart pounded so loudly in her chest she was afraid they could hear it. Did they know what it was to face the threat of losing a child? Did they share the same burden, know the same fluttering of fear in their stomachs? Did their heads throb like hers?

"I don't think I'll go with you right now," Kim said breaking into Laura's train of thought. "I'm not ready to see Shelly yet." Her eyes swam with tears. "I think I'll take a walk." The love ties between Kim and the little sister she'd helped to raise ran deep.

"Are you alright, Kim?" Laura asked, gently touching her arm.

"Yeah," Kim responded nodding weakly, "I'm OK. I just need some time to think, that's all. I want to be by myself for awhile."

She quickly kissed her mom and dad. *How they must hurt,* she thought looking into their tear-stained faces. She turned slowly and walked through the big double doors feeling sick at her stomach with grief.

Inside the elevator Dick pushed "2" and the big metal doors bumped slightly as they slid shut.

"Are *you* OK?" he asked slipping an arm around his wife. He usually felt warm and content holding Laura. Right now all he felt was fear and helplessness. He couldn't ease Laura's pain. He looked down at her, brushing a tear from her cheek. He pulled her closer.

"I'm OK," she said sighing deeply. She wrapped her arm around his waist and laid her head on his shoulder. With her free hand she gently patted his tummy, a family tradition. Michelle's round, smiling face flashed through her mind and another tear slid down her cheek.

God, please, Dick prayed silently as the elevator slowed to a stop at their floor, *make us strong.* He drew in a deep breath, bracing himself. The doors parted with a weary groan and they stepped into the hall just a few feet away from Michelle's room.

A familiar laugh greeted them and they turned to see Michelle rolling toward them in a wheelchair. Her feet stuck straight out in front of her in bright yellow fuzzy slippers. She was flapping like a grounded bird, pushing the chair as fast as she could. Her dark eyes were wide and full of fun; sandy curls bounced around her pink cheeks and wide, infectious grin. She leaned into a quick turn at the end of the hall, her yellow robe adding a touch of spring to a colorless day.

Close behind came Kathy Graham, a widely grinning child in pigtails. Kathy was wheelchair competition for this race and also a patient on this floor. Her blue gingham nightgown dusted the large steel wheels of her chair, revealing long white casts on both legs as she rolled past Dick and Laura, hot on Michelle's tail.

"I'm gonna beat you!" Shelly called over her shoulder.

"You had a head start," Kathy protested giggling, pushing as fast as she could.

Dick and Laura, hand in hand, smiled in spite of heavy hearts.

"Alright you two!" Joy Sutera, the green-eyed Italian nurse, called out as she headed for the girls, her face stern and reproving. But it wasn't hard for Dick and Laura to spot the fun in her large warm eyes. As she passed them she flashed a quick grin, never missing a beat in her pursuit of the racers.

"This race track is closed for the day," she called continuing after the girls. "You nearly flattened your parents at the elevator."

"Aw, Joy," the girls chorused. "Just one more race?—from here to the nurse's station?"

"No!" She was smiling, but the girls knew it was time to quit. "You settle down now. It's almost time for your lunch."

She picked her way between the wheelchairs and started back down the hall. Michelle swung around like an old pro and rolled closely after Joy.

"Can I help with the lunch trays when they come? Can I?" she asked looking up at the pretty dark-haired nurse.

"I don't think so," Joy stalled. "You're supposed to be a guest here." She playfully grabbed Michelle by the chin and looked her square in the eyes, their foreheads touching. "If they find out you're the one who does all the work they might decide they don't need me and I'll be out of a job."

"Hey, Price," Dick said latching onto the wheelchair. "Joy has work to do. Let's go see what we can find in the playroom." He whirled her chair around and they headed down the hall, giving Joy a quick "hope she hasn't worn you out" glance. Joy smiled back at them as she continued toward the nurse's station.

"How come you call me 'Price,' Daddy?" Michelle asked, temporarily resigning herself to adult supremacy. Grabbing the arms of the chair she lifted herself up off the seat as they rolled toward the playroom door.

"Oh, I don't know," he teased, letting the chair free-roll a few feet and tucking Laura's hand under his arm, "it just fits you sometimes."

"I like it," she said dropping herself back onto the seat with a thud.

"What'll we play today?" she asked absently looking over the assortment of toys and games scattered just inside the door. A clutter of colorful boxes, books and toys lay before them.

To Laura and Dick Michelle looked delicate, almost fragile in her soft green nightie and yellow robe. Shelly seriously studied the array of treasures stretching across the room, measuring their worth. The hope of victory in a rousing game of "Candyland" or checkers was written in her eyes.

Dick and Laura's choice would be not to play games, especially now, but Michelle needed a diversion, something to fill some time. She could not guess how ill she was. She didn't know how their hearts ached.

Time, Dick thought watching Michelle carefully unfold a checkerboard. *How much time do we have left with Shelly?* He opened his big hand and scooped up several checker pieces scattered on the play table.

"I'll be red," he said.

Back in the nurse's station, Joy commented to another nurse, "Michelle's a cute kid."

The other nurse looked up briefly from a patient's chart she was writing in and smiled at Joy. "She can sure be a pest though," she replied. "Sometimes I'd like to ignore her, but she won't be ignored."

Joy reached across the counter and picked up a clipboard. She started recording blood pressures and temperatures from a slip of paper she'd taken on her rounds earlier. "She just decides you're her friend, so you *have to* want her around."

"Yeah," the young woman responded closing the metal chart and replacing it in the rack beside her. "Michelle never wonders whether she's welcome."

"Most of the time she's right," Joy added as she finished her list. "I like having her around."

She reached into a white wire basket for the small stack of lab reports just delivered. Leafing through them she stopped at a pink slip from pathology. Michelle's name was on top.

In large, handwritten letters was the word "POSITIVE." Her eyes widened as she took in the next two words, *"Osteogenic sarcoma."*

Numb, she dropped the reports back into the basket and clutched at the chair beside her, lowering herself to the seat. *Cancer!* she thought. *She's really got cancer.* She blinked several times trying to clear her thoughts. *I knew it! Every time I care about a patient it's some awful disease.* She tightened her jaw and clenched her fist, digging her fingernails into the palm of her hand.

She could not believe the flood of emotion crowding in on her. Anger, so much anger. "Why, God?" she called out. The sound of the anger in her voice made her conscious of the others in the nurse's station around her. Her cheeks flushed with rage and embarrassment. *Why Michelle?* she thought. Questions shot through her mind. *How can you let this happen to me over and over again?*

She quickly got up and started into the utility kitchen. Tears stung her throat and she wanted out of the mainstream of activity. She had to be alone.

This is stupid! she scolded herself, shoving a stack of supplies to the back of a counter and knocking them over. *I'm a nurse. Sickness and death aren't supposed to bother me like this. It's part of my job.*

She walked nervously to the door then back again. She thought about the surgeries, the chemotherapy. . . . *They're so sick with chemotherapy, so deathly sick*—She thought about the pain, the risks that lay ahead of this small, smiling child, the little girl she thought was so special.

Shaking her head as if to deny the truth she'd learned, she cried out loud, "I can't watch her go through it!" She clenched her teeth, "I just can't!"

She wiped her nose and her tear-filled eyes as she thought about Michelle, only there four days. But there were few other kids she'd taken a liking to quite so fast. Michelle's warmth and maturity would be a credit to someone many times her age. Her sense of humor kept her own troubles in perspective and helped the other children—and adults—to take themselves a little less seriously. She was exceptional, with the spirit of a champion.

It isn't fair Michelle has to go through this! Joy thought as she slammed her fist on the counter. *With so many self-centered freeloaders in this world, why Michelle?*

She paced the small kitchen like a caged animal. Then carefully, with deepening resolve, she forced her emotions into a protective sheath of indifference. *I'm not going to get wrapped up in her, that's all. I won't let it bother me this time.* She stopped pacing and shoved both hands into her uniform pockets, *I just can't take it.*

She stared up at the big black and white face of the clock on the wall. It was nearly three o'clock, time to go home. Grabbing the pins that secured her cap she angrily pulled it off her head and jammed it into the plastic bag in her locker. Snapping her sweater off the hook and flinging it over her shoulders she walked briskly down the corridor, past the nurse's station.

"I've gotta go," she muttered without slowing down, "something's come up." She pushed open the stairwell door and walked out.

During the 7:00 A.M. briefing the next morning Joy was relieved to learn that it had been arranged for Michelle to transfer to the City of Hope in Duarte, another California hospital specializing in catastrophic diseases. *Good,* she thought, her new resolve still intact. *At least I won't have to watch her go through it. I'm glad the surgery won't be done here.*

A little later, Joy stood before a wall of shelves preparing for her morning routine when a student nurse interrupted her thoughts.

"Joy, I was just in Michelle Price's room and they're packing her things."

Pulling a small stack of bed sheets from one of the shelves Joy said, without turning around, "She's being transferred to the City of Hope today."

"I know," the young woman in the blue uniform continued. "But she's really upset over the move."

Joy wrapped both arms around the stack of linen she held and turned to face the young nurse. Dispassionately she asked, "What's wrong?"

"It's you."

"Me? I haven't even been in there this morning. How could I have upset her?" she said defensively.

"You won't be at the City of Hope when she gets there," the girl went on. "She doesn't want to leave you, Joy."

Joy fixed her eyes on the student nurse feeling like she'd been struck. Waves of compassion, a need to "be there" swept through her. All her defenses weren't enough to keep one small child out of her heart. She handed the stack of linen to the student nurse and walked down the hall toward Michelle's room.

"I hear somebody's been getting tears on my clean sheets in here," she said putting a hand on Michelle's shoulder.

Michelle was lying face down across the bed, but hearing Joy, she turned and threw herself into the nurse's arms. "I don't want to go," she sobbed onto Joy's crisp uniform. "If you won't be there I don't want to go."

Joy held tightly to the little girl heaving great sobs in her arms, and weighed her feelings. She knew there was pain ahead of her if she let herself love this child. She lightly stroked Michelle's back, and tears filled her eyes as she made her decision. "I'll be there, honey," she said. She was opening herself to more hurt than she cared to have, but she knew now it was a risk she wanted to take. "I won't be your nurse but I'll always be your friend. You couldn't keep me away."

"Will you come and see me?" Michelle asked, squatting on her knees on the bed. Never taking her eyes off Joy she rubbed the tears away with the back of one small hand.

"My day off is Sunday," Joy said. "Could I come see you then?"

"Oh, Joy," Michelle grinned, hugging her around the waist, "I can't wait till Sunday."

2
No Hiding Place

Laura sat dozing in a chair, every now and then pulling her head upright as she nodded forward. There'd been so little time for things like sleep in the past week. You simply took it where you could.

With a jerk she startled herself, then sighed wearily as the feelings of fright subsided. The sleep hadn't refreshed her. Groggy and disoriented, she stared through weary eyes at the small bouquet of dainty yellow roses Jim and Linda brought for Michelle yesterday. The miniature buds were easing open in their fluted milk-glass bowl. She could smell their perfume across the room.

Slowly she came out of the fog. She remembered now—Michelle's room, City of Hope. *It must be Thursday . . . or is it Friday?* It slowly swirled back.

It is Friday, she thought. *Yesterday was Thanksgiving Day. It was so strange celebrating a family holiday like Thanksgiving in the hospital.*

She thought about the dinner they'd shared in the play yard. The staff worked so hard to make it nice. Special trims on the trays, little cardboard turkeys and cherub-like Pilgrims smiling up beside the cranberry sauce.

Thanksgiving, she mused. *Sometimes it's hard to be thankful.*

"In everything give thanks. . . ." She'd quoted that verse so glibly before. Now she wondered. "*Everything,* Lord?" she whispered looking at Shelly asleep in the hospital bed. "How can I thank you for this?"

She rested her head against the back of the chair and thought about yesterday. The whole family, even Laura's mother from the east, sitting around the yellow metal picnic table. Kim, her long brown hair shining in the sun, kept Michelle entertained with sisterly teasing and silly jokes.

Michelle looked so pretty in her fancy new blue dress with the ruffled neck and sleeves. She was in good spirits, sneaking the treats from everyone's tray when they weren't looking.

And Rick, broad shouldered and tan—the picture of health in his blue plaid sport shirt—carrying Michelle from place to place, patiently pushing her on the big tire swing.

And then there was Dick, gentle Dick, so open about his feelings, so deeply reflective, so unafraid of vulnerability.

"We might be closer to the real meaning of thankfulness now than we've ever been," Dick had said, thinking out loud.

"What do you mean, Dad?" Rick asked, stopping beside Dick to let Michelle debark from a piggyback ride.

Dick picked up his fork and pushed a couple of green beans around the plate into his mashed potatoes. "Well," he answered thoughtfully, "my Christianity really didn't have much meaning before that awful accident of yours."

"What'd my accident have to do with your faith?" Rick asked, sitting down on the bench with his back against the table.

Dick heaved a sigh packed with deep emotion. He propped his fork on the edge of his plate and looked beyond the fence across the grounds. "Seeing you all cut up and bleeding after the truck hit you on the freeway—" His face flushed and his throat felt tight as all the feelings of that night rushed through him again.

"Oh, Rick," he went on, "you were so bad, the doctors and nurses running around trying to help, trying to save your life. There was nothing they could do."

"But I made it," Rick added.

"Yeah," Dick said raising his eyebrows, "only because God gave you back to us. I couldn't do anything to help you, no one could." He leaned forward, his elbows on the table, his voice quieter, intimate as though sharing a secret.

"Rick," he said looking steadily into his son's eyes, "I *saw* God at work in you." He put his hand on Rick's shoulder. "The doctors said you were going to *die*. They admitted it. There was *nothing* they could do. God healed you, son, and He let me *see* Him at work. I'll *never* be the same. Never. For the first time in my life I saw what it meant to really trust God."

That's so hard to do, Laura thought letting yesterday's memory slip away. She walked to Michelle's bed and slid her fingers around the cold, steel railing, gripping it tightly. Shelly lay sleeping on her stomach, a pale blue blanket drawn across her. Laura reached out and lightly touched the little legs. She shook her head, tears slowly filling her eyes.

"Oh, Lord," she cried quietly, "there isn't any hope. They all agree with Dr. Abrams—they want to take part of her leg or they say she'll die. Please, God, don't let her die."

Limp, she dropped to her knees beside the bed and wept hot, stinging tears. "Oh, Lord," she cried. She rested her forehead against the backs of both hands as she gripped the rail with her fingers. "I know I should trust you, give Shelly to you completely," she paused, trembling as she drew a breath. "But I don't *want to!*" A cry burst from her, the bed shaking with her sobs. Helplessness engulfed her and hopelessness loomed so close. She wanted to strike out and make someone, something stop pulling Michelle from her. She wanted to *do* something to keep her, to force death far away from them. She longed to return to familiar routines—school, work, dirty dishes, each other.

For several minutes she knelt beside Michelle, nauseated and uncomfortably warm, too weak, too drained to get up. She ran her hand under the hair resting on her neck, now wet with perspiration.

Slowly she stood to her feet. "I can't do anything to stop this, Lord" she cried. Shelly stirred and Laura put her hand over her mouth to muffle her sobs. "I can't fight it anymore either," she whispered.

Moving to the chair she sat down and rested both hands on its cool chrome arms, closing her eyes and tipping her head back as if waiting for a downpour of strength.

I can't hold onto Shelly even if I try, she thought. *It's as though I've already lost her. I have no control. There's nothing I can do,*

Lord. You're the only one who can help. She's all yours.

Quietly, the early dawn erased the surrounding darkness. Pale light filtered through the skylight overhead. Shadows lightened and disappeared as warm sunlight slowly streamed into the room.

Deep inside her an assurance came, almost like a voice, "I love her, Laura, more than you do."

Laura's heart was pounding, pulsing in her back against the chair. Her options were clear. She could turn Shelly over to God and trust Him to do what was best, or she could keep fighting Him . . . just as long as she liked.

"I can't fight anymore," she said softly. As a calming peace flowed through her she rested her head against the back of the chair and whispered, "Lord, you can have her back—even to death."

Scraps of a Bible verse she once knew pushed into her mind. *He who began a good work . . . will complete it. . . .*

She couldn't remember the rest but it didn't really matter. She looked at Shelly and turned the words over again in her mind, *He who began a good work will complete it. . . .*

"This isn't something He can't finish," she whispered. "He loves Shelly, even more than I do."

The battlefield within her fell quiet. "No more fighting, Lord."

Peace and refreshment swept over her. She closed her eyes and sighed deeply. For the first time in days she felt rested, able to breathe again. The tenseness slowly left her body as she lay quietly in the warmth of a new and unexplainable sense of security.

The bright sheaths of sunlight soon woke Michelle. She rolled onto her back and slowly blinked her eyes, adjusting to the brightness.

"Well," Laura teased from her chair. "You *are* going to wake up today. I thought you might sleep till tomorrow."

"I might," Michelle said stretching like a cat in a patch of hot summer sun.

"Mommy," she said sitting upright, suddenly wide awake, "can we go home today?"

"Not for awhile yet," Laura answered evenly.

"But I miss my *frieennds,*" Michelle said dramatically emphasizing the last word. Then remembering the puppy Rick said was waiting for her at home she added, "And I'll bet Lady thinks I ran away."

"I'll bet you're right," Laura said moving to the bed and sitting down. "I'll bet they all miss you too."

Michelle snuggled up to Laura and hugged her around the waist, "I love you, Mommy," she said enthusiastically.

"And I love you too, honey," Laura responded. Her voice was light for Michelle's sake, but the words sank deep within her.

Over the familiar sounds of breakfast trays clattering in the hall, Michelle heard Kim and Rick coming in the door. Soon the room was filled with chatter, with everyone warmly involved.

By choice, Dick was not part of the broadening realm of absentee fathers. He'd promised himself he never would be. The uniqueness and importance of all three kids to him and Laura was one of the threads in their strong family ties.

They were a tight unit. Nobody in the family was too busy to take the time when somebody needed encouragement, support or someone to share with. They'd all taken turns staying with Michelle since her illness began. They knew the same supportive love would be there for any one of them if they ever needed it.

"Hey, Michelle," Kim said, "hurry up and get dressed. It's neat outside. Let's go."

Before long Michelle, dressed in a red T-shirt and blue jeans, plopped into the wheelchair and rolled toward the door, grinning at her father. Looking every bit the swashbuckling musketeer, Dick opened it with a flourish and bow. Everybody laughed, and it felt good.

In the hall, antiseptic hospital odors met them, underscoring the reality of what lay ahead. Laura reached for Dick's hand. In the world they created with love and each other, cancer seemed very far away. Walking through these halls they realized it was not far enough away.

As Rick pushed her along the hall Michelle looked into a room where a young boy walked slowly toward the door.

"Hi," she called smiling broadly at him.

He leaned up against the end of the bed, pulled his blue terry cloth robe tighter around him and looked at her without changing his expression or returning her greeting.

She looked back as they passed the door, puzzlement replacing her fading smile.

In a room on the other side of the hall a little preschooler wiggled expertly, protesting the face-washing his mother patiently persisted with. With a "weary-but-loving-it" expression, the mother glanced up as they wheeled by and spoke volumes with her look.

As they turned the corner a young girl near Michelle's age sat on her bed in her room, tugging at an unruly T-shirt, rumpled and clinging to her head.

"See, Michelle," Kim teased, "other people get stuck in their T-shirts too."

The child forced her head through and emerged, free, blonde hair flying in all directions.

"Hi," Michelle grinned, trying again.

The little girl smiled shyly from her bed and dropped her eyes. She was still trying to sort out how to get her arms in her shirt sleeves as Michelle and her family turned the corner and moved through the lobby.

Outside the hospital doors, the rich russet-and-brown painted trees contrasted with deep green spruce and firs on this mild November day.

"Let's play hide-and-seek!" Michelle said.

"How're you going to do that in here?" Rick asked patting the arm of the wheelchair. "Did you forget you have to stay in this thing?"

"You can push me. I'll tell you where," she improvised. "Come on, Kim. You be it. We can all hide in the roses."

"Oh, Michelle," Laura argued, "if we—"

"Come on, Mommy, it's fun!"

Before Laura had a chance to finish her sentence Kim had covered her eyes and was counting, "One . . . two . . . three . . ."

Michelle directed Rick in a hoarse whisper. "Over there, Rick. Over there!"

Laura and Dick looked at each other and shrugged. They didn't feel like playing games but Michelle did. Maybe one round.

Dick felt foolish sneaking around the garden all crouched down. He watched Laura inching between the tall rosebushes hunched over so "it" couldn't find her.

"If I look like that" he thought, "I hope nobody we know comes by." He glanced over his shoulder as he crept along a path and there was Michelle, ducked down in the wheelchair, completely involved in the game. She looked like a small commander of an important secret mission. Her expression made his feeling foolish worthwhile. What looked like a silly child's game to anyone else was really love-in-action to this family.

Michelle seemed to sense the seriousness of her illness, though no one had said anything to her. They kept her waiting, secretly hoping the doctors would change their diagnosis. Maybe they were wrong. But Michelle asked questions—like the one earlier in the week, "You used to be a policeman, didn't you, Daddy?"

"I sure was," he answered.

"They take care of us and protect us, don't they?"

"Policemen?" he asked.

"Uh-huh," she said.

"They sure do."

"And you didn't let the doctors take Rick's leg when it was hurt, did you?" she went on intently watching his face.

Dick looked at her, afraid of what she was thinking.

"You'll take care of me too, huh!" she said confidently.

How could he let her down like this? His stomach churned. He wasn't going to be able to do what she trusted him to do so easily. God knew he tried. Oh, how he tried! He'd done his best. But now he knew his best wasn't good enough to save her leg. The surgery was set for Monday.

All week she had lapsed into short, deep silences—time spent thinking things through—and quickly followed with bursts of activity. Her family recognized her attempt to bury thoughts that surfaced to disturb her. Hide-and-seek was one way she could keep things off balance.

After Kim "found" everybody, Dick and Laura settled on the grass while the kids played on.

"It doesn't seem real," Dick said. "She sure doesn't *look* sick." After a long pause he added, "It's all so crazy."

They sat is silence for a time, alone in private thoughts.

"We've got to tell her, Laurie."

"I know we do," she said watching the kids bobbing through the rainbow of rose blossoms. "I know."

"What day is it?" Dick asked. It's hard to keep track of time.

"Saturday," Laura said breaking off a piece of clover.

"That doesn't leave much time," he said almost to himself.

"What if there's nothing wrong with her?" Laura said. Dick looked startled. "I mean, you said yourself she doesn't look sick. What if . . ." she searched for words, ". . . what if she's been healed? There are so many people praying for her, it's possible, you know."

She looked for Dick's reaction. He was listening, not sure what he thought.

"Maybe," she continued, "we could have them do another biopsy before they—" she paused still unable to say the words.

"We could, I suppose," Dick responded finally. *Another biopsy.* He thought for a minute running his fingers back and forth across his forehead. "But God won't let her lose her leg if she's not supposed to. I mean, something will stop the surgery. A power failure maybe; all the lights will go out."

The thought of doctors and nurses feeling their way around surgery in the dark amused Laura. "They can't operate in the dark," she said wryly. She thought a minute, and added, "Maybe lightning will strike their instruments and they'll be too hot to handle."

They looked at each other and smiled at their fantasy.

"Dick, we're terrible!" Laura said in mock rebuttal. "Poor doctors. I don't wish them any harm."

"Yeah," he mused, "but it'd be worth just about anything if Shelly could keep her leg."

He took Laura's hand. "Honey," he continued, "we're going to have to see this thing through no matter how much we hate it. And we've got to tell Shelly—today."

"I know," she said soberly. "She needs some time to get used to the idea, and there isn't much time left."

She put her head on Dick's shoulder and wrapped one arm around him. Hot tears spilled onto his shirt. "We've got to tell her. But where do we start?"

"I've gone over and over it in my head. I rehearsed different ways with Kim last night. I still don't know what to say."

"Oh, Dick, how can we tell her she'll never run again?"

"It's the hardest thing we've ever had to do, Laurie." He pulled her close and leaned back against the weathered old tree. Tears rolled down his cheeks and disappeared in his beard. "Our only other choice is to tell her she's going to die."

3
Rose Garden Promises

Later that afternoon Dick walked over to the bed where Michelle sat on top of the blankets with her legs straight out in front of her. Kim sat cross-legged on the floor, leaning against the wall. They laughed over a private joke and Shelly grabbed her rabbit, flinging it at her sister. Kim ducked in exaggerated fear.

"Lousy shot," she teased Shelly.

"Honey," Dick said sitting on the bed close to Michelle. "The results are back from all the tests and we want to tell you what the doctors found."

Kim tightened her grip on the floppy stuffed rabbit and stared at the floor. She knew Shelly had to be told but it hurt so much to think of her little sister's pain and loss.

Shelly looked at Dick, studying his face carefully. Then she flopped back against the pillow. She missed the mischief in his eyes and the almost-smile he usually wore when he spoke to her. Twisting a ribbon on the front of her shirt she said, "I want you to tell me, Daddy. Nobody else."

Shelly's request caught Dick off guard. Everything was shared in their family. It was always that way with them. Did she know what he was going to say? Could she possibly sense the seriousness of her illness?

"I have to have Mommy with me, honey," he stammered.

"OK," she said still not looking at him, "but just you and Mommy. Just you."

Dick nodded his head and closed his big hand around both of hers. "OK. It'll be just us."

Ten minutes later, walking out into the sunlight with Laura and Michelle, Dick began to realize how frightened he was. His breathing was fast and shallow, his mouth was dry. He leaned forward pushing Shelly's chair down the walk to the rose garden. That's where she wanted to go, by the waterfall.

He began perspiring in the warm sun. It was an effort just to raise his feet off the ground. *What will I say, Lord?* he thought as they walked through the winding paths. *I can't tell her. I can't.*

He looked away to keep Laura from seeing the tears he couldn't hold back. But she was lost in her own thoughts, feeling the heaviness of the burden they were shouldering together. Tears blurred her own vision fusing the reds and yellows and pinks of the roses around them.

Maybe we should have let the doctors tell her, she thought. *How's she going to take it? Oh, Lord, give us the right words. Prepare her. Somehow help her understand.* She reached for Dick's arm and moved closer to him, lacing her fingers together and pressing his arm against her. She'd never noticed how long these paths were before. It felt like miles right now.

"I hear it, Daddy," Michelle said; "it's over there under those big trees." Turning in the direction of the waterfall the sun warmed the shadows on her face. Her eyes were large and serious. For the first time since she'd found this place she did not seem happy to be here.

As they walked the last few steps to the shaded waterfall, Laura looked up. The sky was blue and the wind was pushing big billowy clouds around. *How can the world still look so much the same? Shelly's losing a leg . . .* She looked at Michelle sitting stiffly in the wheelchair in front of her, . . . *maybe even her life.*

An evergreen canopy shaded the falls and a cool mist filtered down on them, mingling with the heady perfume of the roses.

Dick set the brake on the wheelchair and sat down next to the falls on a short stone bench. Laura took Michelle on her lap and they settled in the wheelchair beside him.

"Honey," he said, trying to find the right words. Pausing, he drew a deep breath, fighting to get enough air. He looked into Michelle's eyes; her face tipped up slightly as she watched his expression intently. She sensed something was very wrong. He knew she did.

"The doctors have studied all the tests they made on your leg," he began, "and they've found out why it's been hurting you so much. There's a tumor in the bone." Michelle's eyes searched her father's as he continued, "There isn't any medicine that can make it better."

"That's why we've taken you to the very best hospitals," Laura said, "and to so many good doctors. We want you to have the best chance you can to get better."

Dick took his daughter's small hand in his. "The only way they can treat a disease like the one you have is to remove the bad bone."

A puzzled look came across her face, "Can they take the bone out and leave my leg?"

"No, honey," Dick said. He wasn't able to say more. His voice broke and he hoped Michelle hadn't noticed.

She caught her breath as though suddenly seized with stabbing pain. "Oh, Daddy," she cried, tears filling her eyes, "I won't be able to dance anymore if I don't have my leg!" The thought gripped her. "I don't *want* to be a *cripple!*"

Wrenching her hand away from her father's, she covered her face, burying herself in Laura's arms. Her small shoulders shook as she wept, the sobs coming from deep inside.

Dick leaned forward, his head in his hands. Tears squeezed between his trembling fingers. "Oh, God," he cried, "I feel so helpless!"

Weeping, sharing a grief they'd never dreamed possible, Laura and Michelle rocked slowly back and forth in the wheelchair, crying softly together. Laura stroked Shelly's soft hair, closing her eyes and pulling her daughter closer to her.

A few long moments passed. Shelly stopped crying and took a deep breath. She pulled away from Laura, straightening up and rubbing the tears from her cheeks.

She looked at her mother's tear-streaked face and a new sadness filled her dark eyes. She reached up taking her mother's face in her two small hands.

"I'm gonna be OK, Mommy," she said soothingly. "Don't cry anymore." Michelle's tenderness made Laura's tears flow faster.

Michelle patted her mother's face and reassured her, "I was scared when Daddy told me, but Jesus made me feel safe inside. I'm gonna be alright. You'll see." She circled Laura's neck with one short arm and they held each other tightly without a word.

"I hate to interrupt," a young nurse said quietly. They looked up at her, their faces wet with crying. She shifted her attention to the pink rosebud she held in her fingers. "I'm sorry to have to break in on you." she went on, "but Michelle is scheduled for x-ray now."

"It's alright," Laura said reaching into her purse for a Kleenex.

"We were having a talk about Shelly's operation," Dick said taking off his glasses and wiping his face.

"I know," the nurse said. She stooped down next to the wheel-chair and held the rose out to Shelly. "I picked this for you."

Michelle took the flower and, with her head down, softly said, "Thank you." The nurse kissed Michelle lightly on the forehead and walked back down the path toward the children's wing.

They collected themselves a little, then started pushing slowly back along the garden path to x-ray.

"Daddy," Shelly asked, turning the rosebud slowly around in her fingers, "why would God let this happen to me?"

Dick and Laura looked at each other, tears welling up in their eyes. *Why indeed. Oh, God, I wish we knew.*

"Honey," he said slowly, "we don't have any idea why this happens to anybody." They pushed on in silence, the muffled sound of rubber tires rolling on cement.

"Maybe I know," Michelle said as they entered the building. "If they don't have any medicine to fix this kind of sickness yet, maybe they can study my leg and find some. Then they can help other kids when they get sick." She glanced up at Laura walking beside her. Michelle looked contented, satisfied. It was answer enough for her.

Dick raised his eyebrows and looked at Laura. She just shook her head in amazement. Love and pride flavored their sorrow.

As they approached the elevator Laura stepped ahead of them and pushed the button.

"Watch this!" Michelle said secretively. The elevator settled on their level. At the perfect moment she dramatically snapped her fingers and commanded the doors, "Open!" They yielded obediently to her magical command.

Dick and Laura thought they saw a little bit of "magic" in the way she was dealing with her loss too.

As they rounded the corner to x-ray a dark-haired, bearded young man wearing a lab coat stepped into the corridor. His badge tapped against the pens in his pocket as he walked toward them.

"Hi, Ron," Michelle chirped.

"Hi, Michelle," he called back. "How are you today?"

"I'm fine. What are you doin'?"

"I'm taking some x-rays in here. You want to help me develop them? I'll be through in a minute." He winked and pushed his way through the swinging door into the treatment room.

"She's going to be here a little while," another technician told Laura. "If you'd like to do something else we'll bring her back to the room when she's finished."

"Thanks," Laura said. "She loves to follow Ron around. But don't let her give him a bad time."

"We won't," the girl said smiling. "She's a big help."

Michelle grinned broadly and scooted a little higher in the chair.

Walking through the underground tunnel from x-ray to the children's wing, Dick and Laura silently pondered the events of the last few minutes. It seemed like a lifetime.

"She sure took it well," Dick said thinking out loud. He wanted to forget all of it, but couldn't. He had to talk, to share the heaviness he felt.

"If I hadn't heard her say what she did about not wanting to be a cripple, I'd wonder if she'd even heard us." Laura thought back, amazed at Michelle's strength and maturity.

"Well, honey," Dick said slipping his arm around her, "we've been praying. Maybe God's answering our prayers by helping her accept all this."

"It's funny, isn't it?" Laura asked looking up at Dick as they walked on through the tunnel. "Her faith has always been so strong. I mean, God's been a working part of her life ever since she was little."

"Do you remember that time she was talking about Jesus coming back?" He smiled thinking about his little five-year-old talking about the second coming of Christ.

"When she told us we should be going to church?" Laura asked.

"Yeah," Dick answered. "What was it she said?"

"Oh, something like, 'One of these days Jesus is coming back and we're gonna be embarrassed 'cause we won't know what to say to Him.'"

Dick remembered. "That's right. She thought we needed to know more about the Bible stories so we would have something to talk to Him about when He comes back."

Laura thought for a minute then added, "Funny part is she was right."

"It didn't take us long to get active in a good church and start maturing in our faith after that," Dick added, a faint smile playing around his mouth.

"Dick," Laura said soberly, "can you imagine going through these last six months without Christ?"

"We'd never have made it, Laurie," he said quietly, "never."

Stepping off the elevator in the children's wing Dick and Laura met Dr. Rose on his way to his office. He was a thin man, quiet in speech and manner, always warm and pleasant to adults and children alike.

"Have you had a chance to talk to Shelly yet?" he asked, matching the pace of his steps to theirs.

"Yes," Dick responded, "just a few minutes ago—in the rose garden."

Dr. Rosen stopped and turned to face the Prices. "How did she seem to take the news?" he asked looking intently into their faces.

"Very well," Laura said with some enthusiasm. He looked doubtful. "Really, extremely well," she added.

"She's her old self again," Dick said. "When we took her to x-ray just now she was snapping the doors open and pestering Ron like always."

"Are you sure she *understood* what you told her?" the doctor asked in a steady voice. He tipped his head slightly and narrowed his eyes adding, "It's very important that she really understands what's happening Monday if we want her to accept and adjust well to the amputation."

"She said she doesn't want to be a cripple," Laura recounted, "and she was upset about not being able to dance anymore." She was slightly unsure herself now in the face of the doctor's questions.

"She even asked us why God would allow this to happen," Dick offered. "She decided for herself, that it might be so you could study her leg and find a medicine to help other children so they wouldn't lose their legs."

"Well," the doctor straightened his narrow bow tie with one hand, "it does sound as if she heard you. But her carefree attitude concerns me some. I don't think she really understands what's happening. I'd like to talk with her too, maybe to answer questions she might have. I'd really like to get a feel of her understanding."

"Sure," Dick responded, "we'd appreciate that."

"Fine then," the doctor said resuming his stride toward his office, "this afternoon, about two? In the conference room." He pointed in the direction of the room he meant and nodded at them as he rounded the corner.

At two o'clock several people began to gather around the chrome-legged conference table in the tiny room. Bright yellow bookshelves lining the wall behind the door were the only color to the otherwise all white room.

Michelle, in a perky yellow dress, sat with her hands in her lap. Her sassy rabbit, tucked snugly into the corner of her chair, peeked out beside her. Dick and Laura sat at the table next to Michelle and Kim settled into the chair on her other side.

Rick still found it uncomfortable sitting for very long, so he chose to stand behind Michelle. As they waited for things to get under way he impatiently shifted his weight from one foot to the other. Everything in him wanted to run as far and as fast as he could, but something constrained him and kept him in the room.

On the other side of the table Dr. Lee sat nodding in agreement to a comment from Dr. Jackson. Dr. Rosen took the empty seat beside Dr. Jackson and laid Michelle's hospital chart on the table. He pulled a pen from his pocket and wrote something in the corner of a small yellow tablet. Laura smiled to herself wondering if the doctor was writing down the final link in a cure the medical world was waiting for, or if he was reminding himself to get a loaf of bread on the way home.

She liked the doctors they'd met here. Dr. Jackson was a thin, attractive woman in her late thirties. Her dark complexion accented large brown eyes and an easy smile. She was friendly and open with people.

Dr. Lee, about the same age as Dr. Jackson, was very efficient in manner and dress. Her sleek shoulder-length hair was pulled back from her face and secured with tiny combs. She was thorough, one who questioned rapidly, and listened intently when others spoke.

Then there was Dr. Rosen. From the first day at the City of Hope Michelle loved him. He was a gentle man with a well-trimmed moustache that moved emphatically as he spoke. Michelle especially liked his warm hands, just a part of his overall warm ways.

Dr. Rosen rolled his pen in his fingers as he said, "Michelle, we know you talked with your parents this morning. Dr. Lee, Dr. Jackson and I wondered if you have any questions you'd like to ask us about your operation."

"Well, yeah," she said reaching for Kim's hand. "I do have one." She looked down at her leg briefly, twisted her foot around slowly. "Is it true I'm going to lose my *whole* leg?"

Dr. Rosen looked at Dick and Laura with an expression of shock. They were just as surprised as he was.

"Where did you get that idea, Shelly?" the doctor asked gently.

"I heard them talking in x-ray. Somebody said my name. They said I was the girl who was going to lose her leg."

Dr. Rosen shot a quick glance at Dick. "No, it's not true, Michelle." The doctor looked at the child across from him and marveled at her strength. She sat quietly listening to his explanation, nodding occasionally, or making a face when she didn't understand something he said. She gave no sign of fear, no anger over the impending loss of a limb, she was not emotional. She held tightly to her sister's hand and accepted information that reduced grown men to tears,

"We want to be sure we get all of that diseased tumor so it can't cause any more trouble. So we'll probably go a couple of inches above your knee. But you'll have a nice long stump so you can use an artificial leg later on. We call that a prosthesis."

"Will you sew the pros . . ."

"Prosthesis," Dr. Jackson prompted.

". . . the prosthesis on my little leg?"

"No," Dr. Lee answered, "your 'little leg' will have to heal first before you can get a prosthesis. Then we'll fit you with one just right for you. It will strap on in a special way and you can use it like a new leg. But you can take it off when you want to."

"Will I be able to wiggle the toes on my new leg like real ones? I like my toes."

Dr. Jackson smiled slightly, "It will have toes but they won't wiggle, Shelly."

Michelle was candid and uninhibited, asking questions for several minutes. The doctors spoke patiently and were thorough in their answers to her.

Finally Dr. Rosen asked, "Is there anything else we need to talk about, Shelly?"

"I was wondering," she began. Then pausing briefly she touched her hand to her hair." "Am I going to lose my hair?"

The room was silent as the adults tried to collect their thoughts. No one had mentioned chemotherapy and no one in the room knew where she might have gotten the idea. It was too soon to get involved in the subject, though. She had enough to accept already. "We'll talk about that later, OK, Michelle?" Dr. Jackson asked gently.

Dr. Lee clicked the point back into her pen. "We've talked about so many things today I'd think you need some time to think about what you've heard."

Dr. Rosen closed the chart in front of him and put the pen back into his breast pocket with several others. "Michelle," he said, "if you think of other questions, I want you to ask me or one of the other doctors. We care very much about what happens to you."

Emptying out of the tiny conference room everyone filed into the hall. As Rick steered Michelle toward the play yard, Dr. Jackson caught Laura's arm. "Mrs. Price," she said quietly, her eyes darker and very wide, "that is a very special little girl. I'll never forget her."

She looked intently at Laura, then self-consciously drew her hand back and pushed it into her lab coat pocket. Turning, she walked briskly down the hall past the others.

4
Before

Dick sat up slowly and swung his feet to the floor one at a time. He leaned forward resting his elbows on his knees, and rolled his head slowly from side to side trying to work the stiffness out of his neck. He rubbed the back of his neck and his shoulder. His whole body ached. It had been a long night. The makeshift bed in Michelle's room had seemed to get shorter and narrower as the night wore on.

He looked sleepily at his watch. Laura and the two older kids were due back soon. He hoped Laura had been able to get some rest. She was looking so tired.

Absentmindedly he rolled the stem of his watch between his thumb and forefinger as he looked over at Shelly. He thought about his family—Laura, with her easy smile and willing attitude. She'd put up with a lot from him in the 20 plus years they'd been married. How many unannounced relatives and needy friends had he brought home that she'd fed and housed without complaint? How many good laughs they'd shared. There would be no way to count.

And there wasn't any way to count the tears they'd shed together either—over the two babies they'd lost, the hard times they'd faced, the tragic deaths of parents, the house fire, Rick's accident . . .

Rick—handsome, strong, eager. Finally pulling a lot of the straggling ends of his life together, leaving behind the adolescent he'd been to become the man he now was. He'd been through a lot.

Dick smiled at his own choice of words, *been through a lot?* If God hadn't intervened, Rick would be *dead.*

That horrible accident. A shudder ran through Dick thinking about it. Rick on his motorcycle, speeding down the freeway. The truck. Every wheel on the left side of the diesel passing across his body. Nineteen thousand pounds of weight on each of the five axles. Dick shook the thought from his head. He couldn't think about his son lying helpless in the road, the crushing weight of that enormous truck. . . .

I'll never forget it. The scene in the emergency room flashed through his mind again.

Rick lay so still on the big hospital cart. There must have been 10 doctors and nurses working in the flurry of action around him; some in white uniforms, some wearing surgical greens, their conversation static and muffled as they scurried around the room feverishly trying to stay ahead of death. They didn't say much but their faces betrayed them, showing how bad off Rick really was.

"Will he live?" It startled Dick to hear himself say the words.

"I wish I could say what you want to hear, Mr. Price," the young red-headed doctor said, stepping out of the activity, away from the table where Rick lay motionless. "He's strong. Awfully strong. The incredible, extensive injuries, the blood he's lost; it's hard to believe he's still alive, let alone conscious."

"That's a good sign, then?" Dick asked hopefully. "His being conscious, I mean?"

"I don't know." The doctor took Dick's elbow and led him to an x-ray viewer mounted on the pale green wall behind them.

"These are some of his x-rays. You can see for yourself, his pelvis is fractured." Taking the black and white x-ray off the monitor he chose two smaller ones from the large pile of films on the table in front of them. Jamming them quickly into the clamps at the top of the viewer, he pointed to the negative on the left. "Here's a view of his left leg, the femur's broken in several places." The doctor turned away from the x-rays to face Dick.

"Mr. Price," he continued slowly, "I can run my hand all the way down the bone inside the muscle of his thigh. I'm afraid he's going to lose that leg." He paused watching Dick closely.

"From what we've been able to see here in the emergency room, all his internal organs are floating." He went on, "The urethra is completely severed, and his bladder is burst. There are deep abrasions on his lower back with openings from inside the body cavity clear through his back. The muscle and tissue on his left buttock have been ground away . . . just gone."

The young man's voice became gentler. "We won't know until we get him into surgery just how extensive his injuries really are, and what we've missed here in our preliminary examination. We'll try our best to save him, but," he paused again and looked at the floor, "it doesn't look good."

"You're not even giving me any hope," Dick said pleadingly.

"It's a pretty hopeless situation." The doctor's voice was compassionate and there was a slight tremor in the hand he put on Dick's shoulder. "He's lost so much blood, Mr. Price. He may not even be able to take the stress of surgery."

Tears welled up in Dick's eyes as he sought strength to sort out what he was hearing, to make decisions that needed to be made for his son. He looked across the room where Rick lay. A pile of ragged, blood-soaked clothes cluttered the floor where they'd been cut off him and dropped out of the way. Rick's boots were under the gurney where he lay fighting for his life.

"I want to talk to him," Dick said moving toward the center of activity. "I want to see my son."

As he and the doctor approached the side of the table a nurse glanced up and stepped back, opening a space where Dick could stand beside the boy.

He looked down into the face of his only son, and swallowed hard. Rick's face was terribly puffy, his eyes nearly swollen shut. He lay naked under strong overhead lights, lacerations, abrasions, gaping wounds covering most of his body. The team worked around Dick preparing Rick for surgery, trying to stop some of the endless bleeding.

Dick drew a deep breath, obviously shaken by what he saw. Someone slipped a supportive arm around him and Dick suddenly noticed how strangely weak his legs felt. He hoped his expression wouldn't let Rick know how little hope there seemed to be, or how hard it was for Dick to look at the ravages of the accident.

Rick opened his eyes and looked at his father standing beside him. "Dad," he said, venturing a weak smile, "some girl in a car forced me into the other lane. I couldn't do anything to stop . . ."

"I know," Dick answered, nodding as he gently touched Rick's shoulder avoiding the abrasions that nearly covered him. "Don't worry about that now. You just get well."

Rick reached toward his father with one hand, but the effort was too great. He let the hand fall limply back onto the sheet and closed his eyes.

Fear gripped Dick like a cold hand. The doctor beside him, wearing surgical greens, reached over Rick, quickly checking his eyes and listening for a pulse. He flashed a quick look at Dick and both men relaxed a little. Rick was still alive.

"Mr. Price," someone said behind him, "we need your signature on these consent papers for surgery."

Dick turned to face a small green-eyed clerk holding a clipboard. They took a few steps away from the others.

"The permission will cover," she continued clinically, reading from the form in her hand, "repairs of internal injuries, closing of lacerations, and amputation of the left leg at the hip."

Dick grabbed the papers from her hand and turned them around so he could read them. "Amputation?" he repeated astonished. "I'm not giving permission to amputate! Not now."

"But, Mr. Price—" the woman persisted.

Overhearing the conversation one of the doctors stepped over to them. "Maybe I can help," he broke in. "I'm Dr. Dixon, Mr. Price. We need your signature to do what has to be done to keep your son alive. Until we get in there we won't know just how extensive the injuries are, and—"

"I understand all that," Dick said forcing a calm tone. "I'll be right here if you need permission for something else." He looked intently at the dark-complexioned man beside him. *These men are all so young,* he thought. *I hope they know what they're doing.*

"But time is of the essence, Mr. Price," Dr. Dixon continued pressing for the signature.

"Then we're wasting time right now," Dick said. He tightened then relaxed the muscles in his jaw, training his eyes on the doctor's. "Look," Dick said in explanation, "from what you've said we're practically working with . . ." the words stuck in his throat, ". . . with a dead man," it came out in a hoarse whisper. "Am I right?"

Crumpling the surgical mask hanging at his neck the doctor lowered his eyes to the floor and slowly nodded his head, "That's right."

"If you don't take the leg right now will it make a difference whether he lives?" Dick asked.

"No, Mr. Price," the young man answered hesitantly, "it won't."

"Then do what you have to do to save him," Dick said, tears stinging his throat. "If he's going to . . ." he swallowed hard, "going to die, let's leave him a whole man."

He could hold back the tears no longer. The young man in green put his hand on Dick's shoulder as Dick stood weeping in his helplessness. They agreed that the important thing was keeping Rick alive. The operative permits were changed and the amputation postponed.

Dick left the emergency room treatment area to find his family. Laura and Kim were sitting in the waiting room, their faces drawn and filled with signs of worry. He watched them search his face for some sign of what was happening as he walked slowly toward them. He opened his arms and Laura and Kim walked inside, close to him. For a moment or two they simply wept.

"Oh, Lord," Dick prayed aloud, "Rick's so bad. You're the only one who can even keep him alive. Help him make it through surgery. . . ." Mid-sentence he stopped praying. Putting his hands onto Kim and Laura's shoulders he gently moved them away from him, where he could see their faces.

"I don't know why I'm saying this exactly," he said, his forehead furrowed, "but for some reason . . ." he paused, "I'm sure Rick's going to be OK. In fact," he emphasized, "he's going to be 100 percent restored." He thought about what he'd just said and what the doctors had been telling him. "Somehow I know he's going to be alright. I have such a peace about it."

The peacefulness spread between them with a special measure of hope as they hugged each other and prepared to wait as long as it took.

Before leaving for the hospital Laura had taken two minutes to call a couple of close Christian friends to ask their prayers for Rick. They, in turn, had set prayer chains of several hundred people praying for God's best in all of this. And before long, friends made their way into the waiting room to wait with them, to comfort in any way possible, just to be there.

Eleven hours later Rick was wheeled into the Intensive Care Unit. His left leg was in traction, a steel pin inserted through his lower leg under the shin bone with cords and pulleys attached to the pin holding his leg high. Tubes,–IVs–ran from everywhere, some carrying glucose and badly needed fluids, others replacing the precious blood he'd lost; still others—catheters—ineffectively carrying off the waste. The urologist told them that Rick's bladder was in such bad shape that to expect catheters to help was like hoping to catch the waterflow from an inverted glass with a single straw in the center of it.

BUT HE WAS ALIVE!

Hours crept by like days as machines beeped rhythmically, pulsing out a copy of Rick's steady heartbeat. Soft, noiseless steps of nurses, moving around the room, carrying out functions to keep death at bay, faded into the dimly lit, too quiet ICU. The stale smell of urine leaking from Rick's broken body forced its way into Dick and Laura's consciousness and, in that moment, it seemed that death stood beside them, its chilling breath blowing across the backs of their necks. A darkness hung in every corner of the room almost like smoke. It was hard to believe that just outside those curtained windows life was being lived by others as though there was no death.

Laura moved to the window next to Rick's bed and pushed back the heavy drapes. Dawn was breaking slowly, the gray sky taking on a soft rosy warmth. It was a new day, the day after Mother's Day, 1976, one she'd never forget.

Later that morning Dick and Laura sat propped against each other in the hallway outside ICU; Kim was sleeping, curled up on the floor at their feet. It had been 72 hours since Rick was brought in. His condition was still unstable, his blood pressure dangerously low and unsteady. There had been no sleep for either Dick or Laura, and Kim had gotten very little, mostly on the floor of the waiting room. Rick's life was still in the balance and none of them could bring themselves to be anywhere else.

Good friends were still praying and a steady stream of visitors had come by to check on Rick and them. From what people said there had to be hundreds of people praying for them. God would answer.

"Mr. Price," the nurse said beside them. They opened their eyes with a start and immediately stood to their feet. It was news about Rick. There had been some kind of change. The excitement in her voice was obvious as the gray-haired woman smiled widely and said, "His vital signs just stabilized. He's going to pull through!"

Dick and Laura hugged each other, with tears of joy and relief streaming down their faces, and the nurse helped Kim to her feet with a self-conscious hug. Their prayers were being answered. Rick *was* going to make it! And to make sure he got well as soon as possible the doctors ordered a couple of pints of whole blood for him. He needed the red cells to speed the healing.

Soon after the blood was started, Dick was sitting outside ICU waiting to see Rick while Laura phoned some of their faithful friends to let them know about the good things taking place, when a different nurse called Dick inside. "I'm sorry, Mr. Price, but it suddenly looks very bad," she said in urgent tones.

He glanced over at Rick's bed. Half a dozen hospital personnel and doctors were working rapidly over Rick, dragging equipment into his cubicle. Confusion.

"What's happened?" Dick asked, his eyes wide with concern and amazement. "Everthing was fine. What happened?"

"The whole blood," she said shaking her head. "He's had a bad reaction to the whole blood he was given."

Dick walked quickly to the foot of Rick's bed and could not believe what he saw. Rick was lying perfectly still, his face red, his eyes closed, his hands and feet red and swollen to twice their normal size. He could feel the heat of Rick's raging fever rising from the bed as he stood there.

The nurses and doctors moved in and out of the space around Rick's bed administering emergency treatment to get the burning fever under control, to reverse the circumstances. Dick saw fear in their eyes as they soaked and changed cold compresses to lay on his head and chest. Without a word Dick moved to Rick's side and took the boy's swollen red hand between his own. Kneeling there beside the bed, in the confusion of tubes and equipment and people moving in and out, he said simply, "God, whatever went wrong with the blood, reverse it and give Rick a comfortable night's sleep."

Before he stood to his feet he felt the fever leave Rick's hand, moving out of it and up the boy's arm. *How funny,* he thought, standing beside Rick and lightly touching his forehead, *I was praying for him just as the fever broke.* He pushed the hair off Rick's forehead and discovered Rick's skin was cool and dry. "I thought a person perspired when a fever broke," he said almost to himself.

"They do," the doctor beside him answered.

"But. . ." Dick said still puzzled, "feel his head. He's cool and dry. Look at his hands," he said picking Rick's hand up off the sheet. "The swelling's gone."

"You're right," the doctor agreed in astonishment as he moved to the foot of the bed to check Rick's feet. "There's absolutely no sign of fever. He was burning up 15 seconds ago. I can't figure that."

"I was praying . . ." Dick paused as the truth began to sink in. "God healed him, just like I asked Him to. God healed my boy." He felt a mixture of awe and excitement rushing through him like a rapid river. God had done *exactly* what he'd asked Him to. He wanted to turn handsprings. "God, you've done what I asked. You took the fever from him. His body is cool. The fever is gone!"

He pushed aside the privacy curtain hanging around Rick's bed and walked, nearly ran out of ICU. Kim sat waiting on the bench outside the door.

"Go sit with Rick," he said not slowing his pace or explaining. Kim quickly turned to go into the room, looking back at her father as he disappeared down the hall.

"Kim," Rick said as she approached the bed, "I think Dad just prayed for me." He seemed a little disoriented. "Something's happening inside me. I feel . . . different, kinda warm and . . . different."

Down the hall, Dick pushed the button for the elevator. *What's taking so long?* He swung around and pushed open the door behind him to the stairwell. Bounding down the stairs two at a time, his excitement grew with every step. "God, it's you!" he said. It echoed off the walls in the stairwell. "You answered my prayer. You're here. You're really here!"

Outside, he paced back and forth in front of the hospital, laughing and crying, half expecting to be dragged off and locked up because of his joy. The only other time he remembered feeling like this was when he was four years old and gave his life to Christ: All the way home he kept feeling like he couldn't touch the sidewalk.

And now Dick thought over what had just happened. There was no doubt about it, the fever was gone. God did just what he'd asked. "I could ask you for *anything* right now, Lord, and you'd do it. I know it!" A picture of the emergency room doctor popped into his mind just then. Rick was lying on the table and the doctor was running his hand "all the way down the bone inside the muscle of his thigh," while Dick stood beside them praying that God would heal Rick's leg. Suddenly in his mind, he saw Rick's leg healed, so rapidly, in fact, that the doctor's hand was still inside the thigh, permanently! Dick laughed out loud at the ludicrous thought of Rick wearing the doctor the rest of his life.

As the strange, somewhat comical scene faded in his mind he was filled with an intense feeling of responsibility. It didn't lessen his joy but opened instead a new focus to him.

"I think Rick needs to see your power, Lord," he concluded. "I love him, and there's nothing I want more than for him to be well and whole, but I want him to know your love and your purpose in this for him." He stood with his hands in his pockets, looking up at the windows of ICU. "I *know* you're here, and I know you're going to heal him, complete and whole. Just take us through this one day at a time, Lord. Let us all see your power, feel your presence. And let Rick know how much you love him."

Dick turned toward the hospital again, satisfied and content with an assurance that brought complete peace in the middle of pain. He'd been with God. God had never been more real to Dick Price.

They all spent that night at home; the last three had been spent in the hospital. When they got back to the hospital the following morning they met Rick's urologist in the hall outside ICU.

"Have you heard the good news?" the doctor asked them, lighting his pipe and looking over his hands at them.

"You mean about Rick's fever?" Laura asked smiling.

"No," he said pocketing his lighter and blowing a puff of smoke out the side of his mouth. "I mean about the catheters working."

Dick and Laura looked at each other, a mixture of "I-knew-it-all-along" and "I-don't-believe-it" written on their faces.

"*Your prayer* . . ." Laura said putting both hands to her face and looking at Dick.

"That's exactly what I prayed for," Dick said almost to himself, remembering what he'd said the day before when he'd asked for God's healing.

"Well, I don't know about that," the doctor continued, "but I came up here this morning to find you and tell you I was taking Rick back to surgery to do some more bladder repair. In light of this happening last night, though, I'm going to wait another 48 hours. If those catheters aren't working right we're going to have to divert that urine flow through his bowel. Without that little sphincter muscle there's really no choice. He'll never control his bladder again without it and we have no substitutes. But we'll see. Forty-eight hours."

Raising his hand in a salute and shaking his head as he walked to the elevator, the doctor left them standing in the hall, the aroma of his pipe tobacco lingering in the air.

Laura hugged Dick tightly. "Isn't it funny," she said, "how we take things for granted until something goes wrong? We haven't been this interested in Rick's bladder since he was potty trained."

All that day and the next the nurses had to change Rick's bed every hour because of the severe leakage of urine he was experiencing through the wound in his back. His bladder wasn't functioning at all and time was running out.

The urologist was scheduled to check on Rick and decide about the surgery within a couple of hours when one of the nurses checked the plastic bags hanging from Rick's bed and discovered the one designated to catch urine was filling. For no apparent reason Rick's nonfunctioning bladder began to operate within minutes of the doctor's deadline. Rick never did have that surgery, yet his bladder functioned normally from that day.

Three weeks after his accident Rick was moved from ICU to a surgical floor where he continued making rapid progress. It was hard for him to accept his limitations as he began feeling better. "Let me get up and sit in a chair," he insisted. "It's silly for you to change my bed with me in it."

Forcing him to stay put, the nurses told him, "You *can't* get out of bed. You're a very sick man, Mr. Price."

"Look," he persisted, "I've had wrecks on my bike before. I'm a fast healer."

"You were run over by a semi-truck," one young nurse finally explained.

Rick smiled wryly, looking at her out of the corner of his eye, "*Nobody* gets run over by a semi and *lives*."

Slowly, as he healed and began to do more for himself, he also began to understand what a miracle it was that he was still alive. As he began to realize how badly he'd been hurt, he saw the miracle God had done in him.

Quietly, Dick reflected on miracle after miracle surrounding Rick: by rights, he should have died on the freeway; instead he was conscious, even able to remember his phone number; he lived through the ordeal of an 11-hour surgery; he'd received 139 pints of blood without ever becoming jaundiced; his ravaged bladder now functioned normally in spite of the fact doctors never found the tiny, irreplaceable muscle needed to control retention; with additional surgery, a 10-inch stainless steel pin in his femur and several skin grafts, he was walking and running on the leg doctors wanted to amputate.

Dick remembered how his own life had changed through Rick's experience. His faith, kind of a "decoration" before, was now vital to him, a part of everything he did.

He stood to his feet and walked slowly to Michelle's bed. She slept, the little girl who brought them so much joy, always singing and telling elaborate, fanciful stories.

Sighing deeply, his shoulders rounded as if bearing a heavy load. "Dear God," he whispered leaning heavily against the railing of the bed, "where does it stop?"

5
And Then There Was One

The sun was warm and a crisp autumn breeze teased leaves off overhanging limbs. It was Sunday, the day before surgery.

"Hurry up, Rick," Michelle complained impatiently. "I want to see the bears."

"OK! OK!" he shot back. "Keep your shirt on. I'm going as fast as I can. You don't want me to run people down, do you?"

"Well . . ." she mockingly weighed the possibility.

"There they are, Shelly," Kim said pointing down one of the tree-lined zoo trails. "There's a big black one in the pond."

"Where, Kim?" she asked craning her neck to see beyond the crowd. "I can't see."

People milled around in front of the exhibit watching the show-off bears doing their tricks for peanuts. Rick finally found a spot beside the guardrail and pushed Michelle's chair in beside it. She grabbed the rail and pulled herself up out of the wheelchair high enough to see the animals in the pit.

"I like it better when I can do my own walking," she said a little irritated. "I can find little places to squeeze into, and I'm faster than you are." She glanced over her shoulder to Rick, flashing an impish expression.

He ruffled her hair and said, "Look at that fat little bear in the corner. He looks just like you."

They moved onto the next exhibit where brown bears were lying in a heap, soaking up the sun. Michelle watched them as they sprawled lazily around the water hole. Two little cubs in the corner cuffed playfully and tumbled together around the sleeping adults.

"I wonder why God let this happen to a rowdy kid like me," she asked indirectly, "instead of some little girl who likes to sit still a lot and read books?"

Before anyone could say anything, a woman standing next to Michelle backed away from the railing, talking to someone, and bumped into the wheelchair.

"Oh, excuse me," she said smiling as she turned to see who she'd walked into. When she saw the short-haired little girl smiling up at her her expression changed, and the smile was replaced with a troubled look.

"I . . . I'm sorry," she said backing off. "I didn't see you there. I'm really sorry," and she disappeared uncomfortably into the crowd.

"She looked like something was wrong," Kim said.

"She sure did," Dick agreed. "Maybe the bears reminded her of somebody she doesn't like."

They pulled Michelle away from the railing and pushed on to the other exhibits. Before long they were collecting reactions to Michelle and her wheelchair. Some people glanced at her dispassionately, then turned to stare after she'd passed. Others coming toward them went out of their way to make enough room for her. Children looked, often asking questions when they didn't understand. Their parents appeared embarrassed and uncomfortable, stammering apologies, sometimes to Dick and Laura, not as often to Michelle.

When someone did ask what happened, Michelle tried to explain about the tumor. But it was clumsy and uncomfortable for her and the person asking. By the end of the morning she had a selection of answers ready. "I hurt my leg," was all that needed to be said, especially to the children. Those who wanted to know more she referred to Dick or Laura.

But the day was beautiful. Autumn smells mingled with the crisp breezes and everywhere they went they laughed. There was a real feeling of closeness and harmony. Laura's mother was with them, and it meant so much to Michelle to have her grandma along.

After the zoo they stopped for an old-fashioned picnic in the park.

They spread their blanket on top of crackly brown and yellow maple leaves dotting the ground all around them, and they took funny pictures of Rick and Michelle and Kim doing "hear no evil, see no evil, speak no evil."

Lying on her back on the blanket with Dick and Laura, Michelle looked up through the skinny fall fingers of the trees over their heads. She said quietly, "I like today. It's been fun." She watched the clouds move silently across the blue sky then rolled onto her stomach with both hands under her chin. "I like being us, Daddy, and *not* being at the hospital."

"Hey, Price," Dick said sitting cross-legged beside her, "is there anything we haven't done today that you think we should have?"

She thought for a minute, then said, "I sure had a good time, but . . ." she scooted herself into his lap and circled his neck with both arms, "there is one thing. We re-e-e-ally need to go to Farrell's."

Farrell's—where bells ring and ragtime music plays, and waiters and waitresses sing "Happy Birthday" over sirens announcing huge portions of ice cream being served to people with insatiable, ice cream appetites. It's a noisy, raucous place that Michelle loves dearly.

Dick and Laura hoped for a little quietness, even solitude, on the afternoon before Michelle's surgery. At Farrell's, both were out of the question.

"You sure that's where you want to go?" Dick asked hoping she'd reconsider.

"That's it," she said putting her nose against his and opening her eyes wide. "Can we, Daddy? Huh?"

Dick grinned melting under her warmth and wilyness. "OK with you, honey?" he asked Laura.

"I guess so," she answered, "if that's really where Shelly wants to go." They took a family vote and Farrell's won by a landslide.

With great fanfare and an honest joy they packed up Michelle and what was left of the picnic and headed for Farrell's. Before long Dick and Laura walked into the restaurant trailed by members of their chattering family crew. The noise level inside was just as they remembered—deafening. From somewhere in the middle of the din a rickey-tick player piano played bravely on unnoticed.

They settled around a table near the center of the room and Michelle turned her thoughts to enjoying herself completely. She clapped and sang along with the music, taking in all the sights. With every bell and siren she loved it more—talking and laughing, eating ice cream and drinking in life.

Most of the people around them were also talking and laughing together. But here and there others seemed lost in their own worlds in the middle of all the confusion. Laura watched one young couple sitting in the corner as they ate their ice cream like mechanical people, hardly speaking to each other between bites. She looked back at her family—happy, animated faces and a genuine caring for each other. Different ages, different personalities drawn together by a common bond—love. No one in the room would guess that in a few short hours this animated little girl across from her would lose her leg. There wasn't a sign from her.

Laura saw a kind of dignity in Michelle she'd never noticed before. At eight years old, still a small child, she trusted Jesus enough to simply *accept* the loss of her leg and give Him the worry. She was honestly enjoying herself the night before surgery!

The ice cream was soon gone, but the glow in Michelle's eyes lingered for a long time. They dropped Laura's mother off at her home and continued along the darkened freeway toward the City of Hope. Kim was teaching Michelle a new song with help from their dad and Rick. And Laura listened, smiling to herself. She was proud of her nutsy children, proud of Dick, and glad to be part of these warm people who loved each other enough to set aside their own pain to help one who hurt more.

Riding along the freeway she looked out at the lights of homes lining the area all around them. *They look like diamonds on black velvet,* she thought. *I wonder if they're really as lovely and beautiful up close as they are from here. Some of those peaceful-looking homes must be falling apart inside, full of hurting people crying because somebody they love has died, or torn apart by divorce. . . . There must be abused, mistreated children in some of them and men or women hiding, afraid of alcoholic partners, maybe even fearing for their lives. Crime . . . drugs . . . hatred . . . loneliness. . . .*

Oh, Lord, she prayed as they sped toward the hospital, *what a pretense we all put up. Nobody in that restaurant could have guessed we hurt the way we do right now.* The silly song the family was singing broke into her thoughts again. The lustiest voice of all was Michelle's.

Tears rolled down Laura's face, hidden in the darkness. *Father, keep my pain in perspective. I want to hear the cries of those around me who hurt so much. Give me peace, and comfort so I can comfort others. Don't let me get so wrapped up in my own pain that I miss theirs. We need each other to get through this. And we need you.*

Laura's thoughts were interrupted when Dick turned the car through the entrance to the City of Hope. Apprehension rode with them, an unwanted passenger—a feeling one gets at the top of a high roller-coaster just before plunging to the bottom. A feeling with many faces and no single name.

The well-lit hospital ahead of them underscored the reality they'd pushed into the background all day. Everyone's secret wish was to wake up and find it had all been a nightmare; but to them reality *was* the nightmare.

Dick steered the car into a parking place near the children's wing, turned off the engine and pulled the keys slowly from the ignition. For a moment they sat in the darkened car, each with his own thoughts, no one wanting to step back inside the world of what was coming.

"I'm scared," Michelle said timidly. She sat rigidly staring into the darkness outside the car. Kim put both arms around her kid sister and held her tightly. She seemed so small.

"Oh, honey," Laura said touching Michelle's hand, "we understand how frightening this must be for you." The words sounded hollow to her as she spoke them. No one knew how frightened Michelle felt. No one could know except Michelle.

Finally with resolute determination Dick tightened his grip on the keys in his hand and opened the door wide. "It's been a great day," he said, his voice too cheerful, "but we gotta get back. C'mon, you guys."

Michelle sat on her bed with both feet straight out in front of her. She stared blankly at her dinner tray on the side table stretched in front of her. Running the tip of her spoon around the outside of the plate, she announced flatly, "I don't like peas."

"You don't have to eat them if you don't want them," Laura said absently, recrossing her legs and sighing quietly as she leaned back in the chair. She reached for one of the many cards standing on the night table and reread it. Michelle wrinkled her nose in distaste as she looked back at the pile of gray-green peas on her plate. She scooped three peas onto her spoon and looked at them closely. Then she turned the spoon around and flipped them into the air.

"I don't like peas," she said again scooping up a half-dozen more and flipping them off the spoon in like fashion. Finally realizing what was going on, Laura jumped up and sprung at the mischievous culprit.

"Mich-elle!" Laura was gifted at packing entire sermons into single words. The spoon clattered onto the thick crockery plate and terror filled Shelly's eyes. She grabbed her throat dramatically as Laura descended on her. Michelle's startled look, added to the electric tension everyone was under, broke everybody up. Laughter filled the room warming the apprehensive chill that hung silently around them.

"Sounds like things are going well in here," the tall man said widening his tiny mouth into a smile. "I'm Dr. Moor." He walked toward Dick extending his hand, "I'll be doing the surgery on Michelle in the morning."

"Shelly," Dick said standing beside her and putting his hands on her shoulders, "this is Dr. Moor. He's going to do your operation."

"Do you know Dr. Rosen?" she asked reaching up and circling one of Dick's fingers with her small fist.

Dr. Moor smiled again, "I know him very well. In fact, he's the one who called me up and asked if I'd come be your surgeon because he likes you so much. So we're going to be sure everything goes well tomorrow for you, Michelle."

They talked for awhile and discussed the procedures. Dr. Moor was at City of Hope on a fellowship and would be working with Dr. Ralph Byron through the entire surgery. His attitude was warm and friendly and Michelle liked him immediately.

After Dr. Moor left, Kim helped Michelle wash up and wiggle into a new pink nightgown with short puffed sleeves. She crawled up on the bed, grabbed Rabbit around the middle and settled back against the pillows. Her feet stuck out below the hem of her gown and she stared down at them wiggling her toes, smiling to herself.

"Can you do this, Kimmy?" she asked spreading all 10 toes apart. She opened her eyes and mouth wide with concentration.

"I'm just not that talented," Kim said settling into one of the rocking chairs. She looked at her sister's small foot briefly, then quickly looked away, forcing the thoughts out of her mind.

"I can do it," Michelle said as she spread wide her little pink toes and wiggled them slowly, watching as they moved back and forth. Her smile faded as she looked at her feet and in one quick motion she pulled the covers up over her legs and curled up on her side.

Dick and Laura looked painfully at each other. As Laura stood to go to Michelle, the door opened and in walked Joy Sutera, their friend from Children's Hospital.

"Anybody home?" she greeted, a smile lighting her face.

Michelle sprang to a sitting position at the sound of her favorite nurse's voice and squealed, "Oh, my old gray elephant! You remembered, you remembered to come!"

She held her arms up and Joy matched her enthusiastic embrace. Michelle clung tightly to Joy's neck as they rocked slowly from side to side enjoying the closeness.

Sitting down on the bed beside Michelle, Joy put her arm around the little girl and they leaned back against the pillows.

"They'll probably chase me out of here for sitting on the bed," Joy laughed, "but it'll be worth it, huh, Michelle?"

"I won't let them chase you out without me." She said snuggling into Joy's shoulder, hugging her again. "I'm so glad you came."

"We couldn't have asked for better medicine," Dick added sincerely.

"Or better timing," Laura said, sitting on the edge of the bed across from Joy and patting Joy's hand affectionately. "We're all glad you came, Joy."

"Well," Joy asked taking a quick look around the room, "how are they treating you, Michelle?"

"OK," she said sitting up, "but I still wish you were my nurse. I can't even race a wheelchair in the halls. They won't let me."

"Imagine that," Joy commented, her smile broadening.

Michelle pulled the covers back and turned around facing Joy, sitting cross-legged. Holding the hem of her nightgown out, she asked, "How do you like my new nightie?"

"It's very pretty! What's it say on the front?" She read, " 'Now I lay me down to sleep, I pray Thee, Lord, my soul to keep.' "

"He will too, Joy," Michelle said, nodding with emphasis.

"You're right, honey," Joy agreed. "When He makes a promise He keeps it, and He promised to stay with us always, didn't He"

"Even in the operating room tomorrow," Michelle said thoughtfully. "I won't have to be all by myself."

Other visitors came and went for a couple of hours that evening and there were numerous phone calls they all took turns answering. The evening slipped by quickly.

Finally Joy said, "It's time for me to go now, Michelle, but I'll be back real soon."

"Don't go, Joy," Michelle cried gripping Joy's hand tightly. "I want you to stay here."

"I'd love to, Michelle, but I can't," Joy answered softly. "But I'll tell you what I can do."

Michelle lowered her eyes in disappointment.

"I can pray for you, honey," Joy continued, "and I'll be doing just that. Everything is going to go exactly the way Jesus wants it tomorrow. And I'll be here with you in my heart, even though I have to be at work."

"I love you, Joy," Michelle said with tears in her eyes.

Joy held the little girl close, rocking slightly Burying her nose in Michelle's hair she said softly, "And I love you too, my little friend."

Good-byes were said around and as Joy approached the door Laura picked up her sweater. "Where are you going?" Joy asked.

"We're walking you to your car," Laura responded, "and it's cold outside."

"You don't have to walk me anywhere," Joy protested. "I'm a big girl. I'll be OK, honest."

"Now," Dick said, "you just listen to your 'mother' and you'll be fine."

Laura teased maternally, "Where's your sweater, young lady?"

"In the car."

"Well, it's not doing much good out there," Laura said in mock reprimand as she slipped her arm around Joy.

Each time Joy visited with the Price family they were becoming more and more a part of her, like adopted parents,and she loved it.

The three of them stood in the parking lot beside Joy's car and talked for several minutes. Dick stood behind Laura with his arms around her most of the time.

"You two are hard to believe," Joy said finally, opening her car door and rolling the window down a couple of inches. "Here we are enjoying each other's company, talking about *my* life. You're supposed to be telling me about *your* problems." Dick and Laura smiled a little self-consciously. "A nurse learns quickly," Joy continued. "Most people in your situation don't want to listen, they want to talk about their fears, about their pain."

She took their hands in her own, "I want you to know something. I've been a Christian a long time, and I've seen Christians under pressure in the hospital. Christ makes a difference in some of their lives, in others there's not much to see. But what He's doing in your lives and in Michelle's is incredible. He's using you in ways you'll probably never know. I came out here hoping to encourage you. I want you to know, I'm the one who's been encouraged."

They shared a warm hug and Dick squeezed Joy's hand tightly adding, "You're family with us, Joy. You're a special friend."

Very early the following morning a nurse walked softly into Michelle's room. Dick and Laura sat in two rocking chairs near her bed. Kim and Rick sat together on the window seat talking quietly.

"It's time for your medication, Michelle," the nurse said waking her.

Shelly, drowsy from medication she'd been given the night before, mumbled, "OK," and obediently rolled over for the shot.

As the nurse finished giving the injection, a man in green surgical clothes, his mask hanging loosely around his neck, walked through the door.

"Hi, Michelle, remember me? I'm Dr. Fisher, the anesthetist." Bending slightly over Michelle he said, "How are you feeling this morning?"

She sleepily opened her eyes and looked into his. They were black and clear and shaded by bushy eyebrows that nearly grew together. "I'm OK," she said to the man. "How are you doing?"

He smiled warmly and began to explain what he would be doing to make her sleep. "Do you understand what we're going to do then, Michelle?" he asked his sleepy patient.

"Uh-huh," she responded, her eyes closed again.

"Do you have any questions, honey?" he double-checked.

"Uh-huh," she said lifting heavy lids and looking right into his eyes, "Do I *have* to do this?"

He drew a slow, deep breath. "I wish I could say you didn't have to," he said taking her hand, "but if we don't get rid of that bad tumor in your leg you'll just get sicker and sicker, and finally you'll have to stay in bed all the time. That would be awful would'nt it, Michelle?"

She looked steadily into his eyes thinking about what he'd said. "I guess it would," she answered finally, "but I don't want to be a cripple." Tears filled her eyes and her chin quivered slightly.

"After you heal from the operation," the doctor reassured her, "we're going to help you find a new leg that will work almost as good as the old one. I don't think you'll be a cripple. You aren't the kind of person who stops trying, and *quitting* is what cripples people, Shelly." He left, nodding to Dick and Laura as he walked through the door. Michelle looked at the closed door for a long time, then shut her eyes.

Before long a nurse and orderly rolled a gurney into the room, up beside the bed. "Time to go for a ride, Michelle," the nurse said. "Can you scoot over here on this table for me?"

They helped her onto the gurney, removed her nightgown and tossed it on the bed. The nurse opened a clean white sheet and draped it over Michelle's naked body. Laura thought how very small her daughter looked lying on the table.

The young orderly in surgical greens raised the sides of the gurney. "You can walk with us over to the other wing if you'd like to," he told the family. "I'm sure she'd like some company," he added maneuvering the gurney out the door and down the hall.

Michelle made groggy attempts at conversation in the elevator but had a hard time keeping her eyes open. They walked silently through the underground passage from the children's wing to the adult wing where surgery was. The big rubber wheels of the gurney made a whirring sound as they drew closer to the end of the underground hallway. Michelle held Kim's hand tightly as she watched the blurred lights slip past overhead. Dick kept a firm grip on Laura's arm.

"You need pictures on your walls," Michelle said loudly. "It's too dark in here."

"That's a great suggestion," her driver said. "We'll have to do something about that."

Approaching the end of the passage he stopped the gurney,

turned to the family and said, "I'm sorry, this is as far as you can go."

"We won't be very far away, honey," Dick said bending over her. "You keep being a great kid. Hear, Price?"

She smiled sleepily at him.

"Don't forget, Shelly," Laura said, "you're not alone in there. Jesus is right beside you." Her voice broke as she quickly kissed Michelle and stepped away from the gurney.

Rick and Kim did their best to send her off with a funny line and a smile, but as the gurney pulled up the corridor Rick doubled up his fist and smashed it into the wall, crying, "Why? Why! It isn't fair!" As the fury inside him began to subside he moved into the comfort of his father's arm. They turned slowly and began the long walk back through the tunnel to the room where they would wait.

Laura looked back down the corridor one last time. She saw the gurney rounding a corner, carrying a very small girl with two legs.

6
Life After Loss

Dick stood at the window of the waiting room looking across the road to the entrance of the building where Michelle was. Through the blinds he could see the fountain in the approach, its three figures—a mother, father and small child—their arms lifted high above them in a joyous expression of family love. Water sprayed around them, splashing into the crystal pool beneath, the mist settling gently on blooming rose bushes and other flowering plants all around.

He looked blankly at the fountain, unable to share its joyful feeling. Finally, he focused on the building where Michelle lay, still and sleeping by this time, under bright lights in an operating room. He knew she was in good hands, the best. But part of his daughter was dying even now as he stood thinking of her, and he was helpless to stop it.

And yet at the same time it was for living that the dying must be done. Without the death of this part of her, she would not live.

What a grim paradox, he thought to himself blinking back hot tears. The bronze statue family caught his attention fully. *There's got to be good time ahead somewhere,* he thought, trying to feel some measure of hope. Tears pushed into his eyes, *Oh, God, there's just got to be.*

From across the room Laura could see dark clouds forming beyond the window where Dick stood. The gray November sky was drab and dismal. She focused just inside the window studying her husband's outline against the gray sky. He looked so worn and tired. His shoulders drooped slightly and he sighed heavily, and often. Her feelings matched the mood she sensed from him.

I feel about as blah as the day looks, she thought sadly. She drew a slow, expansive breath and tried to loosen the tension in her neck and shoulders a little. She realized she'd been "tight" almost constantly since this whole thing began. How long was it now? Two weeks? Only two weeks?

It seemed impossible that just two short weeks ago they'd been leading rather normal lives. No hospitals, now that Rick was well again. No tests or cancer. None of this pain for Shelly. *How can one little girl take all this, Lord?* she wondered. *Maybe Rick's right. It shouldn't have been Michelle.* She thought about what she'd just said, and Who she'd said it to. *I don't mean to tell you how to run things, but. . . .* The hot tears started down her pale cheeks. *She's just a baby, Lord. Her whole life ahead of her. One leg! Oh, Lord, I wish it could have been me instead.*

The tenseness in her shoulders tightened into knots and her head began to throb as she brushed her tears away quickly. "Kim," she said softly.

Kim looked up from a dog-eared *Ladies' Home Journal.*

"Would you rub my neck for me?" she asked hopefully. "I'm really stiff. . . ."

"Sure," Kim said, setting the magazine on the end table beside her and walking behind Laura's chair.

"I can wait if you're reading," Laura added.

"I've just about got that article memorized—maybe even the whole magazine," she responded beginning to move her fingers up and down along Laura's tight muscles. Slowly she began to relax under Kim's touch.

"I think hospitals should keep only new magazines for people," Kim chatted absently. "I read that one when Rick was in the hospital, and it was two months old then."

Dick caught Kim's remark and smiled slightly as he moved to the couch beside Rick. He leaned back against the light green wall and welcomed the coolness. "Things are sure different than they were with you, son."

"Different?" Rick responded a little puzzled.

"Well," Dick said sighing heavily, sorting through his thoughts, "to begin with, we weren't given any choice in whether we would give you up. When we got to the hospital you were already 'gone.' We had to trust God to give you *back* to us."

"And with Michelle," Rick said following Dick's comparison, "we've gotta give her up and she doesn't even look sick."

"Yeah," Kim added. "It's almost like we did it to her ourselves."

Ken and Nancy Millett entered the room breaking the tedious waiting. "You don't know how good it is to see you," Laura said sharing a hearty hug with Nancy.

Dick stood up and wrapped both arms around his friend, "Ken, Nancy, thanks for coming."

"Dick," Nancy said slipping her arm under his and squeezing his hand, "we couldn't have stayed home. You know that."

"I've gotta admit," Ken added, settling onto the couch next to Rick, "we'd prefer being with you at a ball game or over dinner someplace. We're just sorry it has to be for this."

"We know," Laura said. "We'd give anything to change it. But in spite of everything, God's peace is so real to us. Especially to Michelle."

"You know, I was just thinking," Dick said furrowing his brow slightly, "a few years ago Shelly told me something I'd almost forgotten. It makes sense now."

"What'd she say?" Ken asked.

"She said, 'Daddy, something very serious is going to happen to me someday. I know Jesus has something important for me to do.' " For a long time no one spoke.

Laura glanced at the orange enamel wall clock for what seemed the hundredth time that morning. The hands weren't moving fast enough. What was taking so long in there? Where was that doctor, telling them that everything was over, that everything was going to be fine? She watched the gray sky grow darker until rain wept onto the roses outside the window.

They talked easily with Ken and Nancy. It meant so much to have friends sharing their hopes and fears. Sharing some of the things Michelle had said and her attitude of acceptance made the whole thing a little easier. Dick and Laura, without a doubt, were concerned about Michelle's circumstances but they believed and acted on God's promises of provision. Through the whole morning they experienced a deep and continuous peace, almost the same as what they had known when Rick was so ill. There was sadness but an unexplainable peace ran underneath everything. Visitors found themselves buoyed up by the faith they saw upholding this family in their time of need.

Several hours passed before Dr. Moor, the surgeon, pushed the door to the waiting room open and walked in. He still wore his greens but had pulled a white lab coat over them and stood with his hands stuffed in the pockets. A surgical mask hung limply around his neck.

"She's in recovery and she's doing well," he began.

"She's alright?" Laura questioned anxious to hear the words.

"She's just fine," Dr. Moor said reassuringly. "She's a little trouper, that one." He shook his head reflecting on Michelle's cooperative attitude from the beginning.

"The surgery went well," he continued. "We removed the leg four to five inches above the knee joint, just as we planned, and there didn't appear to be any sign of tumor spread. It looks like we got it all but we'll have the lab follow through on that. We'll know more in a day or two."

"How soon can we see her?" Kim asked taking Laura's hand and holding it tightly.

The doctor spoke as he drew the door open again, "You could go back to her room anytime. She'll be there within the hour."

"Doctor," Dick said walking toward the surgeon, "thank you, for everything."

"I'm sure we did the right thing," Dr. Moor responded. "I'd have done the same if she were my daughter." He paused, then added, "I'll be back later to check on her," and he was gone.

"Thank you, Lord," Laura sighed, "she made it! I just hope they got it all."

"Dr. Moor seemed to think they did," Kim reassured. "I don't think we ought to even worry about it."

"Let's not worry about anything now," Rick added. "We've all worried enough today to give it up for good."

"I can't believe how much better I feel just knowing Shelly's OK," Kim said as they made their way slowly through the halls to room

146. "But it's going to be so hard to see her . . . without . . ." She groped for better words, but there were none, "without her leg." Tears quickly filled her eyes.

"Kimmy, you're going to do fine," Dick comforted. "We'll just all have to lean heavy on the Lord for what's ahead of us. You'll make it."

"We're all going to make it!" Laura added softly, putting her arm around Kim.

Waiting in Michelle's room Kim looked around. The ceiling was very high with a large skylight over the bed. She guessed that was because it was an inside room, with the only window looking directly into the nurse's station. Room 146 was one of the rooms where very ill patients and those requiring close observation were assigned, and Shelly would be here for several days.

The oatmeal-colored floor tiles echoed under hard-soled shoes, making the entire room feel somewhat like a stage, with the nurse's station at the window a kind of audience, a fishbowl feeling.

In an hour or so a nurse and orderly worked their way into the room wheeling the cumbersome hospital gurney tightly against the bed. They went silently about their business avoiding the eyes of the family.

Michelle lay sleeping in the middle of the big sterile looking cart, her small naked body draped loosely with a sheet. The color had drained from her face and her eyes were closed. They told them she would be under the effects of the anesthesia for some time yet, slipping in and out of dreams.

Stepping to the head of the cart the nurse deftly shifted the IV paraphernalia from the gurney stand to the bed. The only sounds in the room were the occasional clinking of glass and metal and the sound of her rubber-soled shoes squeezing against the floor tiles.

They saw it at the same time. No one wanted to see it at all, but their eyes were drawn to it. The sheet over Michelle dipped vacantly on both sides of her left leg and silently confronted them. Her leg was really gone.

Laura covered a cry with her hand and turned her face into Dick's shoulder. He slowly closed his eyes, shutting out what he could not bear to see. It was so hard to breathe, and there was a tingling sensation in his chest and at the base of his skull. A heavy feeling sank over all of them like a fog settling on a city, cutting off the sun.

Slumping onto the window seat Kim buried her face in her hands crying without a sound. While Rick stood looking at his small sister, the pain he felt surging within mingled with his anger. He turned quickly and bolted from the room. Outside the door he ran a few feet down the hall, then, overcome with weakness he let himself fall against the wall, dropping his forehead against the cold plaster. His arms stretched upward on the wall as he sobbed, "Why, God? Why Michelle? It should have been me, not her. It should have been me." He cried as he once had as a small boy, letting go the walled-in rage, feeling it turn to grief and finally to a vapor of nothingness that covered over the stinging raw feelings inside him.

In the room, at her bedside, the orderly deftly lifted Michelle from the gurney. His shoulders arched slightly, supporting the little girl in his arms. He'd done it so many times before but every one he'd seen, each child he'd touched this way somehow seemed to touch him too. Perhaps it was their helplessness; maybe they just made him remember that he could be the one who was wracked with pain, or had lost an arm or leg. He laid her on the bed. She sleepily looked up as she sank into the cool pillows. Pain shot through her when her stitches bumped the mattress and her face grimaced in protest; then she drifted silently back to sleep.

She slept most of the day as the family dried their tears and resolved they would grow into the changes that lay before them together. They knew it wasn't going to be easy.

Mid-afternoon she opened her eyes to streaks of sunlight coming through the overhead skylight. She watched as tiny particles danced in the warm cylinders of light over her head. Taking a deep breath, she stretched her ribs as wide as she could. She felt like she'd been sleeping a long time.

Laura sat beside her vacantly thumbing through a children's book she'd picked up to give her hands something to do. As Michelle sighed she looked up. "Well," Laura said closing the book and setting it in her lap, "you're awake."

Michelle looked at her mother and sighed again. Then, as if reality had just pushed an unwanted thought into her mind she blinked and looked away, eyes wide. She tightened the muscles in her cheeks and set her jaw. Grabbing the sheet in both hands she lifted the covers, raised her head and painfully drew her eyes to focus on the bandaged stump at the end of her thigh. Her eyes grew dark as she sank back against the pillow and let the sheet settle around her on the bed.

"Oh, Mommy," she cried closing her eyes. Tears squeezed out under her lids and ran down her face onto the pillow. Laura reached between the side rails for the little hand lying limp on the bed. Michelle was trembling as Laura circled her hand with both of her own and leaned forward, her elbows on the bed.

"It's going to be alright, Shelly," she encouraged. "You'll see." Tears swam in Laura's eyes—*if only she didn't have to hurt so on top of everything else.* "It's going to be alright."

Michelle took hold of Laura's hand and watched the shafts of sunlight again for a few minutes. "I heard the voices in the operating room," she said matter-of-factly. "I saw bright lights when I got on the big table." She turned toward Laura and snuggled into her pillow a little more. "It was so-o-o cold in there," she said pulling the blankets around her chin for emphasis. "But the table was warm, real warm."

"The operating table?" Laura questioned a little surprised that Michelle remembered so much.

"I guess so. I wonder if they heat it for you."

"Maybe so."

"Mommy," she confided, "I was so scared."

Laura squeezed Michelle's hand a little tighter. "I know you were, honey. We've all been scared."

"And I was the only little kid in there. I only saw people with masks on their faces. I couldn't even tell if I knew anybody, except Dr. Moor. He talked to me for awhile." She looked past Laura's shoulder into space. She didn't notice the rest of the family nor their concerned expressions. "I really wasn't all alone . . . Jesus was there with me, I knew He was."

In a few minutes she closed her eyes and before long was sleeping fitfully. She struggled with some unseen predator and made mournful groans in her sleep. Without warning she jerked herself awake, seized with searing pain. The leg they had taken was sending signals to her brain that it was knotted into painful spasms, cramping and pulling at muscles that were no longer there, like someone using both hands to pull her toes apart.

Startled and afraid she pulled her leg upward grabbing at it with both hands. "Oh-h-h," she moaned in pain and fright, "oh, it hurts. It hurts! Somebody's pulling my toes apart!"

Laura pushed herself out of the chair gripped with fear. "What is it, Shelly?" she asked over the painful cries. "What's wrong?"

"My leg. My leg," she cried rolling from side to side, her face lined with pain and perspiration.

"Your good leg?" Laura asked trying to calm the child, trying to understand what was happening.

"No," she cried. "It's all cramped up. It hurts, oh, it hurts." Her face wet with tears, her hair damp with perspiration. The pain was relentless. It seared and twisted, burning its way through her body.

Through the viewing window the nurse on duty knowingly assessed the trouble, pushed away from the desk and reached for Michelle's chart. Then she and the medication nurse each used their keys on the double-locked cabinet that guarded the narcotics. Drawing out the prescribed amount into a sterile syringe and locking the narcotics cupboard, she ran into Michelle's room.

"Here's something for the pain, honey," she said pulling back the sheet. She opened the little alcohol sponge and swabbed an area on Michelle's hip then quickly and skillfully slid the needle into her flesh. The clear medication disappeared under the skin and in a few minutes began to dull the pain.

"Remember what Dr. Rosen told you about phantom pain?" the nurse asked, stroking Michelle's forehead, pushing aside her damp curls. "That's what's happening, Michelle. The nerve endings in the leg that's gone are telling your brain something is wrong, all the feelings are different now. But it takes a long time for the parts in your brain that used to get the messages from your leg to understand that it's not there anymore."

"But I really had a charley horse; I could *feel* it all hard and in knots," Michelle justified.

"I know you did," the young woman answered. "Your brain is all mixed up now, and it will tell you you have charley horses, or that your foot itches, or that it's gone to sleep."

"And that's all in my head?" she asked.

"Uh-huh," she nodded, "all in your head."

"Maybe my foot really does itch," she said half wondering. She paused thoughtfully, "What did they do with my leg?" She looked for an answer in the nurse's eyes.

The uniformed woman swallowed hard and sat down beside Michelle. "Sometimes," she began, "they study a leg or arm to discover more things about the disease."

"That's what I want them to do," Shelly said seriously, "then other kids won't lose their legs. They'll have new medicines instead, to make them better."

"That's right," the nurse agreed, "wouldn't that be wonderful?" She studied her small patient's eyes. She could tell Michelle's question was still partly unanswered, so she continued, "And, after they study it as much as they can they'll bury it, or burn it . . ."

"I don't want them to burn up my leg," Michelle said, shocked. "I want it to be buried."

"Then that's what we'll tell them to do." The nurse stood up, slipping her hand into the pocket of her uniform. "I'll tell them we want them to study it first and then bury it when they've finished. OK?"

"OK," Michelle said, then added as the nurse walked through the door, "don't let them burn it." The look on her face was a mixture of hope and fear. She watched the door for a long time after it closed behind the nurse.

The following morning Dr. Rosen ordered the postop IV discontinued. Karen, the nurse removing the confining equipment from Michelle's arm, said without looking at Michelle, "We're going to get you up and walk you to the bathroom."

Michelle looked a little puzzled but waited to see what was coming next. The other nurse came alongside and dropped the railing on the bed. She helped her sit up and swing her leg over the side.

"The room's going around," Shelly said grabbing the bedclothes to steady herself. "I feel funny."

"You're still dizzy from the medicine you've been getting," the nurse said as she wrapped an arm around her tiny patient and eased Michelle to the floor.

Karen moved in close to Michelle's other side, "Just hold onto us. Hold tight."

Michelle wrapped an arm around each nurse's waist trying to gain her balance. The nurses stepped away from the bed and as Michelle tried to catch up to them she automatically shifted her weight to take a step. But she cried out as searing pain shot through her from the newly severed muscles. Without her viselike grip on the nurses she would have fallen. The pain was incredible as she tried earnestly to hop between her escorts; she felt and looked awkward lunging toward the bathroom, clinging tightly to the uniformed women beside her. Frustration and pain filled her eyes as she remembered that only hours before she would have been able to run these few steps from her bed without thinking about it. But she was so limited, so dependent. She felt helpless and embarrassed.

Dick and Laura watched, struggling to hold back their tears. Kim left the room.

"Why don't you and Mom take a walk too?" Rick suggested. "I'll be here if Michelle needs anything."

"Thanks, son," Dick said taking Laura by the hand. "We could use a break. C'mon, honey."

They walked down the hall to the family kitchen. Dick pulled open the refrigerator, took a bottle of pop out and set it on the sink. Laura reached for the paper cups at the bottom of the dispenser and folded her arms holding the cups against her shoulder.

"She looked so . . . awkward, so pitiful," she said looking at the floor, "like a clumsy little bird."

"She'll get better at it," Dick said without looking at her. "It's only her first try."

"I know," Laura said, disagreement in her voice. He took the cups from her and poured them each some of the 7Up he held. "I'd feel awful if she knew how I feel right now," she said, absently watching the bubbles rise and burst at the surface inside the cup. "She'd really be hurt if she knew how hard it is to look at her like that," she added with frustration.

"She doesn't need to know," he said. "She's a strong kid, Laurie." He took her arm gently, "A lot like her mother."

Laura looked at Dick and realized she hadn't focused on him or anything else for a long time. She was glad she had Dick with her in this. They seemed to complement each other most of the time, one was up when the other was down. She wondered how anyone made it through this kind of thing alone, or without God to give meaning to the senseless things that happen.

She set the paper cup on the counter and put both arms around her husband. Neither of them said a word. They didn't need words.

As they walked slowly back into the hall they saw Kim quickly turn the corner into Michelle's room ahead of them. A child's cries met them as they started back down the carpeted hallway.

"Was that Michelle?" Laura asked. They both quickened their pace knowing it was her cry. Pushing open the door on a dead run, they saw Michelle writhing in agony, twisting and turning in a private phantom hell. Sitting beside her talking gently, soothing her little sister, Kim stroked Michelle's back and neck while Rick stood close by, his concern written in his eyes.

"Let's try something," Kim said. "I'm going to rub the leg that's gone."

"You can't," Michelle said squeezing her eyes tightly, then opening them, curious in spite of the pain.

"Let's pretend. Let's play like it's still there, and see if I can rub the pain away."

"It's the back of my leg," she said willing to try anything that would bring relief.

Kim rubbed the back of the imaginary leg, stroking and kneading a badly cramped muscle. Amazingly, Shelly felt some relief. Experimenting in the next few days, they found that when the missing leg itched, scratching the other leg in a corresponding spot sometimes stopped the sensation.

"You've got the magic touch, Kim," Dick said as he watched Michelle relax with Kim's patient massage and quieting influence.

"Yeah," Michelle said, breathing easier, "you're pretty good."

Nurses encouraged her to get up and move around more and more, which Michelle was eager to do. Being sick was never something she took to kindly.

By the third day after surgery she was spending time in the hospital playroom. Bookshelves lining the walls were filled with books for all levels of interest and ability. A blue rug covered the biggest section of the floor; white tiles set apart the game area. The white modern furniture was scaled down to the size of the small-fry patients who used the room, and bright-colored cushions were scattered around on the chairs and floor.

Michelle arranged herself at the pedestal table in the center of the carpet and was coloring a springtime scene with an assortment of felt-tip markers on a page of one of the giant coloring books. Laura was curled up on the other side of the table in a comfortable rocker upholstered in a warm blue fabric. She watched as Michelle, absorbed in eliminating black and white, suddenly shifted her attention.

Glancing down at the bandages taped over the end of her stump, Michelle raised her short leg, gently resting it against the edge of the table. With a dark marker she sketched eyes, a nose and a wry little smile onto the white bandage, then laid the marker back on the table. She looked at the little face for a moment then pulled the leg against her, circling it with both arms and rocking back and forth, humming a lullaby as if she held a baby.

"Is that your baby?" Laura asked.

"This is 'little leg,' " Shelly answered. Lifting it high so Laura could see, she pointed to the marks she'd drawn. "I gave it a happy face. It looks like a baby."

Dr. Rosen simply shook his head when Laura told him what Michelle had done. "That's incredible," he said. "It's usually a period of weeks, sometimes even longer before an amputee will even look at himself, let alone begin to *accept* the changes. Three days! It's really hard to believe. She's accepting everything so quickly. It's almost as though she accepted it before it happened."

A smile crept across his lips as he pictured Michelle with her arms gently holding the stump, rocking back and forth, showing her acceptance and courage. "This is one little girl who's going to make it!"

7
A Newborn Sparrow

Five days after surgery Michelle's progress was rated as excellent. The wound was healing well, her spirits were good, she was handling the nearly constant bouts of phantom pain better all the time and was requiring less pain medication. It was a positive picture except for one thing: this was the first day of chemotherapy.

"Usually," Dr. Rosen told Dick and Laura as they shared a cup of coffee, "we administer Methotrexate, the medication Michelle will be getting this time, in milligram doses. We're giving her a gram dosage, a thousand times greater than what we give adults."

"Why so much," Dick asked, understandably worried at the unusual dosage. "Isn't that a lethal amount?"

"The cancer in her body is a killer. It spreads fast and when it strikes it hits hard and quick." Dr. Rosen ran his fingers slowly through his dark hair, carefully choosing the best words to answer Dick's question. "It is a lethal dosage, Mr. Price, but this medication in any amount is potentially destructive. That's why we follow it closely with an antidote to neutralize the effects of the Methotrexate before it has a chance to destroy healthy cells."

"What can we expect?" Laura asked looking steadily into Dr. Rosen's eyes.

He returned her intensity over the top of the little dark-framed Ben Franklin glasses he wore. "You will see her nauseated, and vomiting. She will experience chills and possibly trembling. Later on she may lose her hair."

"Will it grow back again?" Dick asked.

"Sometimes it does, other times it doesn't. It will depend on many things."

"If she's bald she'll look like a little newborn sparrow hopping around the house," Laura said, picturing Michelle without her hair.

The doctor looked at these two people he had spent so many hours with in the past two weeks. Laura and Kim had been there nearly the entire time, while Dick and Rick came as much as possible around their jobs. There were times when they had been afraid but they were always willing to ask questions, to learn what they could to help Michelle. They were grieved and yet able to direct their love to others around them who hurt also. So many families came here and built cocoon-like barriers around themselves. This family worked hard to keep others close to them, to keep their own pain in perspective with the rest of the world.

"Without chemotherapy," Dr. Rosen said compassionately, "we run the risk that wild cells may have broken away from the tumor before we got it. They could attack her lungs, other bone areas, even her brain. We can't take chances like that with Michelle." He added thoughtfully, "We just can't risk it." He did not wait for them to speak, but stood and quickly walked away.

"Michelle," the curly-haired man said pulling a chair closer to her bed later that morning, "I'm Dr. Kramer. We're going to start your chemotherapy today." He took her hand in his and patted it.

"Let me explain how all of this works," he said gesturing toward the IV apparatus brought in a few minutes before he arrived.

"I already know about IVs," she said quickly. "I've had them before."

"Good," he said, nodding approval. "Then all that's different is how the medicine we're giving you works. "You're getting a medicine that's going to go through your whole body hunting for bad cells that might have gotten away from the tumor before we took it. The medicine will catch those cells and destroy them."

"Like my cat does with a mouse?" she asked hesitantly, a little puzzled.

"Yes, exactly like that," he agreed. "That's a very good way to put it."

He explained that the first medicine would be given some time to work alone, then she'd get a second medicine which would stop the first one before it could hurt any good cells. "All this is a little bit like a war inside you, and you may feel very sick for a few days. We'll do our best to help you feel better as soon as possible.

"Now," he said walking the equipment over to her bedside, "do you have any questions you want to ask me?"

"How long do I have to have the IV?" she asked sitting up. "I can't use my arm good when it's taped on that board."

"You'll probably feel like resting most of the time, but we'll take it off as soon as we can," he answered, opening a sterile needle. "It's going to be several days though before we can do that."

She shrugged and made a face but did as he asked. He took her hand in his and began swabbing the skin over the vein he'd chosen. "Did I answer your question?"

"I guess," she answered watching him push the needle under her skin. "But I'd rather be riding a horse."

"Do you have a horse?" he asked, attaching the IV tubing and taping it in place.

"Not my own," she said settling back against the pillow, "but I'm going to raise horses someday, and I'm gonna be a famous trick rider."

"You know what," he said, tapping the IV bottle with his index finger to start the drip, "I'll bet you make it too."

He stood beside the bed double-checking the apparatus and timing the drip until it was operating the way it should. Each drip falling through the tubing triggered a small regulator making a sub-dued beeping sound. He set a box of tissue and a blue molded emesis basin beside her pillow in easy reach. "I'll be back to check on you in a little while," he said, winking at her over his shoulder. Then he slipped out the door.

Michelle watched the yellow liquid dripping slowly through the clear plastic tubing from over her head. The beeping was slow and even as the fluid ran slowly into her arm. She lay very still for several minutes before she quietly said, "Mommy, I feel funny."

Laura sat down beside her on the bed just in time to grab the emesis basin and hold it while Michelle lost her breakfast. Then suddenly she was gripped with driving pains in her stomach and chills that ran through her body so strongly she shook the sturdy hospital bed like an earthquake. In pain she drew her knee to her chest and held it tightly against her stomach. Laura was amazed at how rapidly the medication had reacted in Michelle and even though Dr. Rosen told them what to expect she was gripped with panic and fear at the signs of the child's violent illness.

"Dear Lord, help her," she prayed, tears rising in her eyes. "She's so sick, Father. Please help her make it through this. Help me to know what to do to make it easier for her."

The next few days were more of the same. Michelle remained violently ill, vomiting, chills, sieges of trembling. The light hurt her eyes and she asked to have the drapes pulled all the time. As Dick sat beside her in the darkened room she woke from a restless sleep.

"How you feelin', honey?" he asked, moving beside her on the bed and putting his hand on her shoulder. She'd been so ill she was losing weight and her little arms seemed smaller than ever to his big hand.

"Doin' OK," she answered. Always "doin' OK," in case she'd make someone else feel bad.

"Daddy," she said in a half-whisper, "did I ever tell you about my dream?"

"What dream is that?"

"I had a dream for a long time that someday I would be Miss America or somebody." She paused and grimaced as the pains began again in her stomach. "I guess I'll have to find a new dream now," she said sadly. "I don't think Miss America ever has one leg."

"Torture, that's what it is," Laura said, tears spilling down her cheeks. "She just lies there with her eyes closed in that dark room. She's been vomiting four days. It's got to stop. How much more can she take?"

"I know, Mom," Kim said, holding the outside door for Laura to walk through. "It's so hard to watch her lying there. She just takes it. I wish she'd have a fit or throw a temper tantrum. It would be easier for me to handle." Kim's own eyes swam with tears.

"Four days," Laura said again, going back over the long hours in her mind. "If she's not better tomorrow I'm going to . . ." Her voice trailed off as a lump formed in her throat. What could she possibly do?

It always upset Kim to see her mother cry. She glanced at Laura and made an attempt at changing the subject. "She sure seems to brighten when Dr. Rosen or Dr. Moor comes by to see her." She thought for a moment, then added almost under her breath, "If it was me I'm not sure I'd be so happy to see them."

"Yeah, she really seems to love them," Laura added as they walked into the cafeteria, "the very men who took her leg."

They stood in silence, their arms around each other. Kim blew her nose and patted at her eyes with a tissue. Laura was lost in her own thoughts as they selected their salads and took a table. "You know, honey," she said, shaking salt on her lunch, "we asked the Lord to heal Michelle hoping she wouldn't lose her leg."

"But He didn't do that," Kim said wondering where Laura was leading.

"But I think He's done something else we asked Him for," she added sounding excited. "I think He's given her a special ability to accept what she has to go through instead."

"You know, I think you're right. How else would she be able to love the very people who make her hurt?" Kim added in agreement. "In fact, everybody I talk to around here asks about her and they all make some sort of comment about her 'spirit,' how positive she is."

"Uh-huh," Laura said, thinking about it, "I've noticed that too."

Kim tapped her straw on the table pushing it up through the paper wrapper. "Last night one of the doctors wanted to know what you and Daddy did with her to make her take it so well."

"What'd you tell him?" Laura asked.

Kim looked at her mother and made a face, "Well, first of all, *he* was a *she* and I told *her* I didn't think you did anything out of the ordinary. We've all been raised to trust God to take care of everything in our lives, and that's what Shelly's doing."

Laura set her fork on her plate and dabbed the corner of her mouth with her napkin. She looked at Kim, "How'd she take that?"

"Oh, you know," she said, looking out of the corner of her eye to demonstrate the doctor's response. "She was a little skeptical."

They smiled together. "It's funny, isn't it," Laura added, "how just simply trusting God never seems like enough of an answer to be an answer?"

"You know," Kim said, absently stirring her coke with her straw, "last night I was sitting with her after you and Daddy had gone and I had my eyes closed. I guess she thought I was asleep and she started praying. Remember how you told her about the goldfish being sick at home?"

"Uh-huh."

"Well," Kim continued, "last night she said 'Dear Jesus, will you take care of the disease our goldfish have? If you don't, I'll understand.' " Kim looked away and continued, "Then she got kind of quiet and said, 'And Jesus, about what I have, take care of my disease. If you don't, I'll understand.' "

They sat in silence for several minutes, then Kim said in hushed tones, "I don't know how anybody gets through something like this without Him. I'd go crazy."

Laura reached across the table for Kim's hand. "Honey," she said quietly, "as long as we've got God we can make it through anything we have to. But I'm glad you're here too. Your faith through all this and with Rick has helped keep Daddy and me strong. We love you, Kimmy." Kim squeezed Laura's hand in response. It was good to breathe deeply together.

When they walked into Michelle's room a little later, Dr. Moor, on his evening rounds, was sitting with his legs crossed on the edge of Michelle's bed. He seemed to be enjoying her animated and continuous chatter.

"So you think you're feeling better tonight," he said, listening to her heart with his stethoscope.

"I *know* I am," she assured him quickly. "Know how I know?"

He shook his head looking very serious.

"I've been thinking about *eating* something," she said, dramatically hoping he'd be glad to hear her appetite was returning. Kim and Laura glanced at each other excited by the obvious change in Michelle.

He was indeed glad to hear such good news. Taking the earpieces out of his ears and folding up the apparatus, he asked, "Something like what?"

Michelle slipped the stethoscope out of his hand and moved

closer to listen to the doctor's heart. "Like a Popsicle or a dish of ice cream maybe." Tired from the exertion of sitting up she leaned back against the pillows and slid down under the covers. With the cold chrome disk on her own chest she listened intently.

"Everything OK?" he asked as she handed it back to him.

She nodded looking very important, "And *your* heart is very good too."

"Well, that's good to hear," he responded, standing to leave, and smiling at her warmly. "Maybe even deserves an ice cream celebration. I'll see what I can do."

"I'm not going to have chemotherapy anymore, Dr. Moor," she said looking up at him.

"Oh, really," he said looking a little surprised. "When did you decide that?"

"I don't need it anymore," she continued, "I'm all well now."

"How do you know that, Michelle?"

"Because," she said choosing her words precisely, "Jesus told me I was going to be all well. He's healed me."

The surgeon sat back down on the bed and spoke gently and directly, "Michelle, it's very hard to go through chemotherapy. You don't suppose that you . . ." he searched for the right words, "If you were better you wouldn't need any more treatments, right?"

"Right," Michelle answered. "But, Dr. Moor, I didn't say that because I don't want any more treatments. I said it because Jesus told me I'm well."

"I believe you, honey," he said gently, "but I think we'd better go ahead and finish the chemotherapy anyway, just to make real sure we've done everything we could to help get rid of the cancer. Jesus could have made you completely well already, but I think He'd want you to finish the treatments."

"OK," she said sliding further down the pillow, "but I'm already better, you'll see."

"Have you told Dr. Rosen about this?" Dr. Moor asked, standing again to leave.

"No," she said seriously, "he wouldn't understand."

"Why not?" he asked surprised at her comment.

"Because he wouldn't believe the part about Jesus. He's still looking for the Messiah, you know."

Dr. Moor clung to his composure until he was outside the room but broke into a hearty laugh when he was far enough away. *What a girl,* he thought shaking his head, still smiling. *I hope she has been healed.* Soberly he thought, *We just can't lose this one.*

The lab technician who had come several times a day for the past five days appeared at the door before breakfast one week after chemotherapy was started.

"It's me again," she said flashing a wide grin at Michelle. She was a pretty black girl Kim guessed to be in her early twenties.

"You sure must like blood a lot," Michelle teased, watching the technician tie the rubber tourniquet around her upper arm.

"Well," she said over the needle cap she held between her teeth momentarily, "nobody's supposed to know this, but I'm a vampire." She smoothly slid the sharp needle under the skin and into the vein, then released the band holding back the blood flow. Pulling back on the plunger she looked Michelle in the eye and made a scary face.

"I already knew," Michelle said trying not to laugh. "But I'm gonna call you Dracula from now on."

The syringe was full and the technician moved expertly through the final steps of the test. "Oh, no," she mockingly pled, "if you do that everyone will know my true identity."

"That's what you get for being a vampire, Dracula," Michelle grinned.

"Guess so," she said moving to the door. "See you later."

She stepped outside, then peeked around the door and added, "Oh, by the way, Dr. Rosen said if this is the right flavor you can go home today. How about that?"

The report came through showing that medication levels from the chemotherapy were in a safe range. About 10 o'clock, Dr. Rosen pushed open the door to Michelle's room, smiling broadly.

"How would you like to take your parents and go home for awhile?" he said taking her hand.

"Can I really?" she asked almost afraid to believe what she was hearing. It had been a little over four weeks since all this began. "I feel like I've been here forever."

"I'll bet you'll be glad to see your own room again, won't you?"

Michelle flung back the covers and reached up to the doctor's shoulders. Holding on with both hands she stood on the bed beside him and threw both arms soundly around the man's neck.

"I can't wait," she squealed excitedly. "I can't wait!"

Pulling into the driveway Dick barely stopped the car when Michelle had the door open wide and was standing outside balancing in the wedge of the door.

"Give me my crutches," she pressed in her excitement. "Hurry, Mommy. Lady hasn't ever even seen me. Give me my crutches."

"Just hold your horses, Price," Dick said, pulling the emergency brake into position and getting out his door.

"I'm doing the best I can," Laura said. "You have to be patient."

"I'm *not* a patient anymore," she said pumping toward the front door, her empty pant leg flapping wildly, "*I'm home!*"

"I meant . . ." Laura started to explain, but gave up and leaned against the seat watching Michelle enthusiastically working her way up the walk she had always run before. A sting of loss pierced Laura's happy aura, but only for a moment. Michelle was home and that was all that counted.

"You alright, Mom?" Kim asked, coming back to the car.

"I'm coming," she answered. "I'm just getting my breath."

Lady was excited about meeting Michelle, and from the first minute she was Michelle's dog and faithful friend, a sturdy collie mixture whose favorite pastime was thoroughly licking Shelly's face anytime she got the chance.

"Let's take her for a walk, Daddy," Michelle said, already hopping after the bright new leash.

"Don't you think that's a little bit too much for your first day home?" he cautioned.

"Please?" she begged. "Mommy, tell him it's OK. We won't be gone long, just down to the end of the street and back. Please?"

"You'll take it easy the rest of the day then, OK?" Laura bargained.

"OK!" she chirped, dropping to her knee beside Lady to fasten the leash to her collar. Lady gratefully licked her face and wiggled in anticipation.

"Alright, but just our street," Dick said offering Michelle a steadying hand. "*You* may feel like a hike, Price," he teased as they stepped onto the porch, "but I'm an old man, and I'm tired."

Shelly manuevered down the path, leash and crutch in her right hand, tugging at Dick's slowness with her left.

As they swung onto the sidewalk and began their way up the street several neighbors were watering lawns or hauling empty trash barrels back into their yards. Friendly hellos were shouted but no one seemed to have the time for the usual chat a walk always produced.

"Daddy," Michelle said on the way back to the house, "I think they feel uncomfortable because of my leg."

Dick responded, a little surprised at his daughter's intuitive comment, "I think you may be right."

Dick listened to the unevenness of the crutch sound and Shelly's one shoe as they walked a little way in silence.

"Daddy," she asked as they neared the house, "will you take a walk with me when you get back from work tomorrow?"

"Sure, honey," he said turning up the walk. Lady slowly followed, unwilling to end their walk so soon. "Lady didn't get enough today."

"It's not for Lady," Michelle said thoughtfully. "I want to go around to the neighbors and tell them what happened to my leg. Maybe they'll feel better then."

He turned to say something but Michelle had dropped her crutch in the entryway and was hopping toward her room with Lady hot on her heel.

"My animals," she cheered loudly, "I've missed you, all of you!"

8
Maiden Flight

As Dick turned off the car ignition the next evening, Michelle burst down the walk toward him.

"Are you ready?" she sputtered. "Can we take our walk now?"

"Does Mom know we're going?" he asked, hoping for at least a short delay. He was not looking forward to this "walk."

"She knows, and she said dinner will wait." She'd covered all the angles as usual. "Come on, Daddy, let's go."

They crossed the street and approached the shrub-lined walk together. The single-story stucco house seemed suddenly unfamiliar and foreign to Dick just now, despite the fact he'd lived across the street some 13 years.

"You don't have to say anything if you don't want," she reassured him, pressing the bell twice.

"Hi, Mrs. Nelson," she called out as the lady opened her front door. The pleasant looking woman stood slowly drying her hands on a kitchen towel as she listened to Michelle.

"I just wanted you to know I had a tumor and they had to take my leg off. But I'm OK now and I'm going to get an artificial leg pretty soon." She smiled at Mrs. Nelson not noticing the look of bewilderment and delight playing across the woman's face. "Oh," Michelle added, "and if you want to ask me any questions it's OK." She smiled at her neighbor as she pivoted and started back down the walk past

Dick who smiled quietly back at Mrs. Nelson still standing on the other side of her screen door.

"Well, thank you, Michelle," Mrs. Nelson said pleasantly. "I really appreciate your telling me all this."

"Oh, it's OK," she responded. "I just didn't want you to worry."

"I'm very glad to hear that you're so much better." Mrs. Nelson waved good-bye and stood thoughtfully watching them walk down her path to the sidewalk.

They visited several houses on their block and then turned back toward home. Dick put his arm around Michelle. "Honey," he said with tears in his eyes, "you're OK in my book."

"Daddy," she said looking up at him, "you're not going to *cry*, are you?" There was almost a scolding in her voice.

"Nope," he said composing himself, "but I want you to know I think you really helped some people with your visits. It's going to make it easier for them to accept you and not feel sorry for you."

"I don't want anybody to feel sorry for me," she said shaking her head, "*I* don't feel sorry for me. I'm just the same, only I have one leg now. Daddy," she added in suspenseful tones, slowing her pace, "when Jesus told me He made me well?"

Dick nodded his understanding.

"He told me something else too."

"What else did He tell you?" he asked.

She weighed the words because of how important they were to her, "He told me He has something very special for me to do with my life. Something very important."

They turned up the walk and Lady bounded down to meet them. "I'm sure He does, Michelle," Dick said thoughtfully. "I'm sure He does."

A few days after Michelle came home from the City of Hope, Kim walked by the bathroom and glanced in the open door.

"What are you doing?" she asked Michelle, who stood in front of the sink maneuvering the medicine cabinet mirror and her head back and forth.

"No wonder!" she said emphatically getting a good view of the back of her head.

"No wonder what?" Kim asked. "What are you doing?"

"Aw, Debby just called me Fred."

"Fred? Why?"

" 'Cause she says I look like old bald Fred Mertz on the Lucy show from the back," Michelle explained matter-of-factly. "You know what?" she said, looking at the shaggy ring of hair still hanging on around the the bald spot on the top of her head.

"What?" Kim asked.

"She's right, I do look like Fred from the back." She swung past Kim and out the front door to find her friends.

In a few days her hair was gone, completely. Now, hopping around the house, she looked very much like the gangly newborn sparrow Laura had predicted.

Her second Thursday home Michelle propped herself in the bedroom doorway as Laura finished dressing. "You going to Bible study?"

"Uh-huh," Laura said, picking up her hairbrush. "Want to come along?"

"OK," she said, watching Laura's hair fall softly as the brush moved through it.

She moved in front of the mirror beside Laura and turned her head from side to side viewing it from all angles. "I miss my hair sometimes," she said, "but I don't mind being bald. I think I have a nice head."

Laura dropped a bath towel over Michelle's face and said, "It's sure getting big enough. If you're going with me you'd better get dressed."

The women in the Bible study group were delighted to see Michelle. They asked questions and talked with her and Laura, catching up on things they'd missed over the weeks.

"We've been praying for you, Michelle," one gray-haired lady said with tears in her light blue eyes.

"Thank you," she answered sincerely.

"You know, Laura," a younger, red-haired woman said to Laura as though Michelle weren't in the room, "I still have a hard time understanding how God could allow Michelle to be handicapped like this for the rest of her life."

An uncomfortable silence pushed against them as each one dug within herself for some sort of answer.

"But I don't think I'm handicapped," Michelle said surprised to think anyone else saw her that way. "Handicapped," she continued slowly and thoughtfully, "is when you can't do something because you're scared, or when you can't love somebody 'cause you didn't get enough love when you were a kid. Everybody's got handicaps like that. I'm missing a leg, and that just shows more."

As they thought about what Michelle said, expressions of pity and remorse changed to understanding and agreement as the truth of it began to sink in. One heavy-set lady circled Michelle with her large arm and squeezed her tightly.

"You're exactly right, honey," she said, her head bobbing up and down in agreement. "Some of us are handicapped a whole lot worse than you are. Other people just can't see it, that's all."

After a rich Bible study Laura and Michelle headed for the shopping center to treat themselves to lunch. As they walked through the shopping center, Laura began to realize her bald-headed, one-legged little girl with no eyebrows or lashes was attracting a lot of attention from large numbers of shoppers. People stared as they saw her coming toward them, even turning to watch her walk away.

"That little boy's missing a leg," she heard some say.

"Did you see that bald-headed kid back there!" one aghast woman said loudly to her companion.

"He must have had lice," another woman explained knowingly to her friend. "Why else would they shave his head like that?"

Michelle heard the comments and saw the stares but kept her eyes on the restaurant door and never slowed down. Laura felt her face getting warm as embarrassment began to push through her.

"What'd you do to your foot?" the waitress asked, noticing the crutches beside Michelle and making an attempt at pleasant conversation.

"I had a tumor," Michelle answered, "and they had to take my leg off."

"Oh," she gasped dropping a fork. "I didn't know. . . ."

"It's OK," Michelle assured her, shrugging her shoulder and glancing at Laura.

"Don't worry about it," Laura assured the young woman fumbling with her order pad and pen. "Kids with crutches usually have a cast somewhere. You couldn't know."

The waitress took their orders and gratefully left the table. Michelle sat rubbing her hands.

"Do your hands hurt you?" Laura asked.

"Yeah," she answered, pointing to the heels of her hands, "right here. The grips on my crutches rub in the same place all the time."

"That'll probably build up a callous after awhile," Laura encouraged.

"Then my hands will look like my feet," Michelle added, "and I'll have *three*."

"We'll have a hard time finding shoes to fit them," they laughed heartily together enjoying each other's company.

"Michelle," Laura asked, arranging her napkin in her lap, "does it bother you when people stare like they do?"

"I don't like it very much," she shrugged, opening her eyes wide and taking a sip from her water glass.

"I think they haven't seen a little bald kid before," Laura said. "What do you think?"

"Yeah," she said making a face. "If I was a hundred years old and wrinkled up they wouldn't even look at me."

"They might think you're Telly Savalas," she teased.

"Who's that?" Michelle asked.

"Never mind," she said pushing some of the cold moisture down the side of her water glass with her little finger. "I just had an idea."

"Oh-oh," Michelle quipped.

"Would you like to get a wig?" She moved her water glass away from her, watching it pull the ring of moisture after it on the formica tabletop, waiting for Shelly's response.

"A wig?" Shelly repeated leaning forward on both elbows and staring at her mother.

"Yeah, you know, hair."

"I don't know," she said screwing up her face again, "I guess."

They ate their lunch and were standing at the register as Laura paid the bill when a young woman and her small son walked up and stood beside them.

"Who stoled your leg?" the little four-year-old asked Michelle, watching her empty pantleg move as she started to walk away.

Michelle looked back to answer his question but his mother jerked him around and slapped him in the arm.

"Don't say things like that," she growled, apparently suppressing a desire to scream.

The child stood crying against his mother's skirts as Laura and Michelle walked out.

"Why did she do that?" Shelly asked upset because the little boy was punished for his curiosity. "He only wanted to know what happened."

"I know, honey," Laura comforted, "some people don't handle these things very well."

"I'd rather have him ask me questions," Michelle said, "than have people sneak looks and not talk to me."

Things lightened up again when they settled down in front of the mirrors in the wig shop. Michelle's natural "ham" instinct flourished as she tried on wigs that made her look like a pint-sized country western singer. Platinum coiffures piled high over a face that looked like Puck and Shirley Temple rolled into one brought giggles from Laura, Michelle and more than one salesclerk.

They settled on a brown short-haired, feathery style and left the store with it sitting proudly on Michelle's shiny dome. People stared less until the wig pitched low over one eye. She reached up to straighten it and quickly had the bangs fringing her ear.

"Here," she said stopping in the busy shopping mall and grabbing the wig firmly on top, pulling it straight up and off. "Put this in your purse or something."

"I can't believe this," Laura gasped trying to catch her breath. The expressions of horror and delight on people passing by added fuel to her fire. "I can't remember when I've laughed so much."

Laura stuck the fuzzy cap into her purse and Michelle snapped it shut with emphasis. Still laughing they headed for the car.

The three weeks Michelle was home seemed to go too fast. Too soon for everybody, it was time for her to return to the City of Hope for the next course of chemotherapy.

Shelly packed her suitcase quietly, folding things neatly.

Back at the City of Hope, Chris, the Children's Wing admitting clerk, put Michelle in a wheelchair and pushed her down the hall toward her old room. Michelle looked through the open door at the empty bed.

"You won't have to be in there this time," Chris said. "That's only for our surgery patients, when the nurses have to watch them real carefully. You're not going to be one of those this time."

They walked further down the hall past a room where a little blonde girl about Michelle's age was lying on her bed. Michelle smiled at her then remembered she'd seen her here once before. "Hi!" she called cheerfully. They pushed around the turn in the hall and into Michelle's new room.

"It's 158 this time," Chris said as she squatted down and lifted the metal footrest on the wheelchair, helping Michelle step out and over to a chair. The furnishings of the room were similar to her old one but much more cheerful, Michelle thought. There was carpet on the floor and a big window that opened onto some of the biggest, oldest trees on the grounds in a spot called Pioneer Park. The rose gardens Michelle loved were just beyond the trees.

"I like this room," she told Chris looking around, as Dick and Laura came in behind them. On the sliding glass doors at the foot of the bed life-size cartoon characters frolicked across the glass. Yogi Bear smiled back at her.

"That's beautiful!" Dick said walking to the window. "Come see, Shelly," he motioned for her to join him. She hopped to the window seat and climbed up beside him. "Look over there," he pointed.

She pressed her nose flat against the cold window pane. "The rose gardens," she squealed, then added wistfully, "I love those gardens."

She'd barely had time enough to put her pajamas on before Dr. Kramer with his curly brown hair and gentle ways came dragging his IV equipment behind him into the room.

"Hi, Michelle," he greeted her.

"Hi, Dr. Kramer," she said enthusiastically, then paused and quietly eyed his equipment. "We gonna start already?"

"I'm afraid so." He pulled the rack beside him and unhooked it from the stand, pulled the stainless steel pole apart from the wheels and slid it into the IV rack at the head of her bed. She watched his every move, sitting midway down the bed, her robe pulled around her tightly.

"You ready?" he asked quietly turning to face his small wide-eyed patient.

"I guess so," she said. She unbuttoned the top buttons of her robe and slipped it off. Pulling the cover and sheet down she slid under the cover and settled against the pillow, her left arm lying on top of the blanket waiting for the IV.

"You're one of the best patients I've got," Dr. Kramer said. He looked down at her through his thick glasses and she smiled weakly at him. He was awfully nice, but she was not looking forward to another bout with chemotherapy. "This time," he explained as he positioned the IV needle in her vein, "you're getting a different kind of medicine. Last time you got the—"

"Yellow kind," Michelle volunteered.

"Right," he said smiling. "That's called Methotrexate. This time you're getting one called Adramycin. It's red. See?" He held the vial up in front of the window so she could see the clear red liquid. "I'll put this into the bottle of dextrose and water here," he tapped the container at the top of the pole on her bed, "and you'll be done when it's empty. With that part of the medicine anyway.

"After that's gone a nurse or I will come in and give you several injections of another kind of medicine to stop the Adramycin. We'll do that every three hours at first for a couple of days, then every six hours for awhile."

"That's a lot," Michelle said biting her lower lip.

"It is a lot," he agreed. "Do you think we can make this if we try real hard?"

Michelle thought about it, then slowly nodded her head, "I'll try."

"I know you will, Michelle, and I know it's hard to do." He looked at her for a minute, then took a deep breath. "Well, shall we get this over with?"

Michelle nodded and watched while he injected the entire vial of red liquid into the bottle over her head.

"See you a little later, honey." he said at the door.

"Dr. Kramer?"

"Uh-huh?"

"Would you turn the lights off, please?"

Laura stood beside the window seat and began to draw the curtains closed again.

"I like to see the trees, Mommy."

"OK, honey," Laura responded. "Whatever helps."

For a long time Michelle looked out the window and watched the trees moving slightly in the wind outside her window. Jays darted from tree to tree looking as if they were hiding something from each other. Before long the sickness struck again and Michelle lay trembling curled into a ball, holding her stomach. Once in a while she would open her eyes and look longingly at the trees. When she shut them again she seemed a little more relaxed.

Late the next afternoon Michelle's door opened and a nice looking man dressed in a dark blue suit stuck his head into the room.

"Michelle?" he whispered.

She was in the room alone, and opened her eyes slowly. "Hi, Pastor Callen," she said weakly.

He walked into the room and sat on the chair beside her bed. "How are you?" he asked in a quiet voice.

"Doin' OK," she said, then reconsidered. "I feel real sick."

"I'm sorry you feel bad, honey. We just wanted you to know we're all praying for you. We love you, Michelle."

As he stood to go a wave of nausea hit her and she grabbed the emesis basin and vomited as he waited beside the bed. He lightly touched her shoulder, then turned toward the door.

"Pastor," she called after him, "I'm sorry you came all the way out here and I couldn't talk to you." She wearily closed her eyes, then opened them again. "Thank you for coming."

He looked back at her with tears in his eyes as the door closed silently behind him.

The effects of the chemotherapy were violent again this time, but by the end of the fourth day they began to wane. She was sitting up in bed, entering into conversations a little more. Everyone breathed a little easier as she showed signs of getting better.

On the fifth day she thought she felt well enough to pull on her robe and crutch her way up to the desk to "visit." She deeply disliked staying in bed. As she rounded the bend in the hall she saw the little blonde girl she'd remembered from the last time.

"Hi," she said walking into the girl's room and up to the bedside. "I'm Michelle," she said smiling wide. "What's your name?"

The little girl looked at her for a long minute, then looked up at her mother beside her.

"Kaylene," she answered hesitantly in a quiet voice.

Kaylene watched Michelle carefully without responding to her friendliness. Her short blonde hair was thinning and getting shaggy like Michelle's before she lost it. Her eyes were large and searching as she sat propped against the pillows on her bed trying to figure out this bald-headed child with the happy attitude standing beside her.

"How long you been here?" Michelle asked.

"A few days before you," Kaylene answered softly.

"This is my second time here," Michelle said with the air of one who knows the ropes. "I have to come back for chemotherapy, but I don't have to have any more operations."

"Is that what happened to your leg?" Kaylene ventured.

"Uh-huh, I had a tumor on the bone." Her new friend seemed uneasy with what she said so she softened her statement, "But it wasn't so bad. I can do lots of things now I couldn't do when I had two legs."

"Like what?" Kaylene challenged.

"Well," she said using her hands to emphasize the words. "I can put my bathing suit on without taking my pants off first." She grinned broadly, "Can you do that?"

Kaylene's mother put her hand to her mouth to hide her delight.

"And my mom and dad are going to take me to Colorado sometime to learn how to ski."

"You can't ski," Kaylene said emphatically. "You only have one leg."

"People with one leg can ski," Michelle explained evenly. "Lots of people do it, I bet.   Well," Michelle said leaning on her crutch, "I gotta go now. I'm visiting. I'll come see you again."

She worked her way to the door then turned and called back, "What grade are you in?"

"Third."

"Me too." And off she went toward the nurse's station.

Kaylene sat looking after Michelle for a couple of minutes. She looked puzzled and confused. "Mommy?"

"Yes?"

"What's she got to smile about?"

Later, after dinner that evening, Dick and Laura were slowly walking the familiar halls while Kim entertained Michelle in the lobby with a game of "Candyland." Kaylene's mother saw them and stepped into the hall as they passed.

"Excuse me, are you Michelle's parents?"

"Yes," Dick said. "We're Dick and Laura Price."

"I'm Dottie Hall, Kaylene's mother," she said motioning toward the room behind her. She was a young looking woman, thin and attractive, a few years younger than they were. "Michelle came in this afternoon while she was visiting and struck up a conversation with Kaylene."

"She wasn't pestering you, was she?" Laura asked concerned.

"Oh, no," Dottie smiled, "just the opposite." She looked from Laura to Dick and decided to say more. "Kaylene has a brain tumor," she began.

"Oh, I'm so sorry," Laura interrupted touching the woman's arm gently. "That must be very hard."

"We're just learning what we're dealing with now that we're here at the City of Hope, so . . ." she paused, and took a deep breath. "Yes, it is hard, not knowing, all the tests . . ." She looked at them again and the worry lines around her eyes softened a little. "But then, you must know exactly what I'm talking about, with Michelle's tumor and all she's been through."

"It's been pretty rough at times," Dick admitted.

"She's got such a positive attitude," Dottie continued, "and she really seemed interested in Kaylene. My daughter hasn't stopped talking about her all afternoon."

"We're glad it helped," Dick said.

"Every little bit makes it easier," Laura added.

"This is the first positive experience she's had since we admitted her to the hospital. She's just gone inside herself in fear. I couldn't thank Michelle enough." She turned to leave, then added, "Will you let her come visiting again? . . . Soon."

"Oh, she'll be back," Laura laughingly assured her. "You can count on it."

Sunday morning Laura left Dick with Michelle and drove to church. It was good to be with their friends again. They asked about Michelle and said that they'd been praying. She wondered if their faithful friends knew how much it meant to them as a family to know that they were being held before God in prayer because of love.

Through some long and difficult nights it was this that kept them going.

Settling into the pew with some friends Laura prepared herself to be encouraged, to be strengthened and prepared again to return to the unknown things ahead of them.

As the pastor spoke he said, "I had a lesson this week in love and what it really is. I drove to the City of Hope on Friday to see little Michelle Price." Laura sat up straighter in her seat. This was the first she'd known of his visit.

"What I saw was a child in tremendous physical pain. She's weak and hurting. Her bed shakes with chills and she's constantly nauseated. Michelle was too sick to talk with me, so I told her how much we love her and about our prayers. As I walked out the door she taught me something about love. 'Pastor,' she said, 'I'm sorry I can't talk to you after you came all this way. Thank you for coming.' "

Laura felt tears stinging her throat. She hardly noticed that people all around her were in tears. "In all her pain," the pastor continued, "she cared enough about me to think how far I'd come to see her. She felt badly that she couldn't talk. What would our homes be like if we loved like that? That's the love of Jesus in action!"

In the car on the way back to the City of Hope Laura pushed an Evie Tornquist tape into the tape deck. As she drove she reflected on what the pastor had said. Michelle seems to give without being concerned whether you can give anything in return, even in her pain she still cares for others.

Then the words of a song caught her attention:

Knowing you'll love me
    through the burdens I must bear,
Hearing your footsteps
    lets me know I'm in your care.
And in the night of my life,
    you bring the promise of day.
Here is my hand. Show me the way.

"It's so clear, Lord," she said out loud, "your care through all of this. You will get us through the burdens we have to bear now—especially Michelle, she needs your strength."

When I think I'm goin' under,
    part the waters, Lord,
When I feel the waves around me,
    calm the sea.
When I cry for help, oh, hear me, Lord,
    and hold out your hand.
Touch my life. Still the raging storm in me.

"The storm that's raging in her body, Lord, hold out your hand to her, give her the calmness in the middle of all this that only you can give. Hear her cry for help and answer her."

Knowing you'll love me
    helps me face another day.
Hearing your footsteps
    drives the clouds and fears away.
And in the tears of my life,
    I see the sorrow you bore.
Here is my pain. Heal it once more.[1]

"That's what the pastor heard wasn't it, Lord? And the doctors and nurses who keep asking why she's accepted all this so well—it's your footsteps, isn't it? Your way of showing us that you're in all of this. Use the pain she's going through to teach her of your special love. Teach all of us."

She rewound the tape and played the song again and again until she turned the car into the long driveway at the City of Hope.

Note

1. Charles F. Brown, "Part the Waters." Copyright 1975 by Word Music Inc. Used by permission.

9
Airborne and Soaring

A full year passed. A year filled with learning and adjustments for all of them. Rick was married to a young woman named Brenda and they were expecting their first child, a documented miracle baby because of the nature and the extent of Rick's injuries. Kim graduated from high school but decided to wait a year before starting college until things with Michelle settled down more.

Michelle was still having chemotherapy treatments every three weeks, and was almost used to comments about her baldness and being taken for a boy. Between treatments she sprouted a little timid fuzz on her head, an encouraging sign that she just might grow hair when all of this was finally over.

Monthly x-rays had become routine for her, regular probing to see whether the disease had spread somewhere else in her body. But reports kept coming back clear. Michelle was doing well.

She tired easily and was quickly bothered by heat, but resumed her usual activities and typical pace very soon after coming home. Her "little leg" slowed her down some, not much.

They had been so busy meeting doctors' appointments and treatment schedules that several weeks after surgery Laura still hadn't been able to get rid of a few things she feared would remind Michelle of her two-legged days. Late one afternoon while Michelle was playing next door, Laura lifted the garage door and went in scanning the contents for Michelle's bicycle, skateboard, skates and other things she wouldn't be able to use now.

A noise behind her drew her attention and her mouth dropped open in amazement. Whizzing past the house, crutches held high at the sides, Michelle sped down the sidewalk on the skateboard Laura couldn't find. Within seconds she returned and passed the garage again, this time squatting on the board with Lady in front as the motor, pulling Michelle uphill.

Laura blinked, then threw her hands up in surrender. "OK, Lord," she said walking back into the house, "you'll just have to keep an eye on her. I can't run that fast."

It was decided at dinner that night that the family ski trip they'd been putting off until Michelle could handle it could probably be safely scheduled. The dates were set, and in a few weeks tightly packed suitcases were sitting at the door ready to be loaded into their camper the next morning. Together they settled in front of the TV to relax before getting to bed. The program they chose was a heart-gripping story dealing with the death of a child. As it progressed Michelle threw herself against Dick and buried her head in his shoulder. "I don't want to die," she sobbed, holding onto her father tightly. He wrapped his arms around her and let her cry for several minutes. She hadn't cried this way since the rose garden, when they told her she would lose her leg.

"That's silly," she said composing herself slowly. She wiped the tears from her face with the back of her hand. "I'm not going to die."

"Michelle," Dick asked gently, "are there things that bother you that you haven't told us about?"

"There's lots of stuff I haven't told you," she said her eyes lowered. "I tell Jesus lots of secrets when I'm having my chemotherapy. It's not stuff you shouldn't know or anything, just . . . sometimes it's easier to talk to Him."

Early the next morning they loaded suitcases, equipment and provisions into their little Chinook camper and took off for a ski weekend at Snow Summit. Chains were required a few hours away from home and new fallen snow covered the landscape with a soft blanket of white as far as they could see.

They found a parking space in the crowded lot at the foot of the slopes with time to spare before they were to meet Michelle's instructor. Before long they were bundled and strapped into everything they needed against the weather and ready for a day of skiing.

"Hi," he called shooshing gracefully up beside them. He moved so easily on skis it was several minutes before anyone noticed he was missing a leg. "You the Prices? I'm Paul." His nose and cheeks were red from the cold and his blue eyes sparkled as he talked about Michelle's background with Dick and Laura.

"Has she skied before?"

"Just once," Dick answered. "We went as a family last year and loved it."

"Great," he said with a big grin. "We'll see you later." Paul handed her two aluminum ski poles with short skis at the bottom, called outriggers. He helped her position her skis and snapped the grips securely on her boot before they took off together for the intermediate slopes.

He sent her down the mountain just ahead of him, calling encouragement and directions about balance and turns as they descended.

"That was great," he commented to her in short gasping breaths. Flipping up the short skis at the bottom of his outriggers he dug them into the snow with a crunching sound. "You sure you're not a professional three-tracker?"

She grinned back at him, "Nope. I only skied that one time before I lost my leg," she said warming her nose with her mittened hand.

Paul looked a little puzzled. "You mean, this is the first time you've used outriggers?"

"Uh-huh," she said nodding.

"And I sent you down the intermediate . . ." He rolled his eyes, grateful she'd made it down unhurt and excited by the expertise she'd shown on her first run. She was a natural.

"She's a natural," Paul told Dick as they took their parkas off beside the fire later that afternoon. "She really did well this afternoon. She learns fast, her balance is great, and she's not afraid of getting hurt. I think she ought to be competing."

"What kind of competition are you talking about, Paul?" Michelle asked nursing a cup of hot chocolate with both hands. She snuggled next to Kim on the couch by a crackling fire.

"Same kind normal skiers do, only you'd be in a class of women and girls who've been skiing about as long as you have. They're all handicapped in one way or another." He pulled his knit red cap off his head, shaking his light brown, tight curls. He flicked his cap and the fire sizzled as bits of snow and ice melted in the flames.

Michelle took a sip of her chocolate and let the warm steam curl up onto her cold nose and cheeks. "I'm not ready to race anybody," she protested. "I'd never make it."

"Yes, you would," Paul assured her, dropping into a chair next to her. "You're good, Michelle, and you've only skied one day. I've seen a lot of handicapped skiers and I'm telling you, you're good."

Late February, 1978, they pulled out of their driveway in Riverside, California with their little white Chinook bulging. Taped along the side was a colorful sign some friends made for Michelle showing Snoopy standing proudly on skis beside bold letters announcing, "MICHELLE IS ON HER WAY TO THE HANDICAPPED NATIONALS, WINTER PARK, COLORADO!"

Two days later, stiff and tired, they pulled slowly up the hill to the center of activity. Stepping from the camper Michelle stood very still, slowly taking in her new surroundings. Like a wide-eyed fawn trying to decide whether it was safe, she leaned forward on her crutches and looked up at the lodge where they would stay.

It was a rambling wooden building, the roof covered with several inches of snow. Icicles hugged the eaves, and snow had fallen not long before they arrived; there was an inch of brand new snow on the stairway and handrail.

She turned to her left and looked down the hill into the little valley below. Several small buildings were scattered around, many with bright red, yellow and blue signs posted against the dark siding. Ski racks opposite the lift area made a dotted line for several feet. The skiers bobbing around in their bright colored ski jackets gave the scene a carnival flavor. Yellow lift chairs silently sailed up and down the mountain, many carrying skiers to the top. Michelle noticed that several of the people sitting in the chairs high above the snow had single skis dangling beneath them flanked with outriggers on either side.

On the other side of the valley, soldier pines stood at attention. It looked like a scene from a bakery store window: everything was

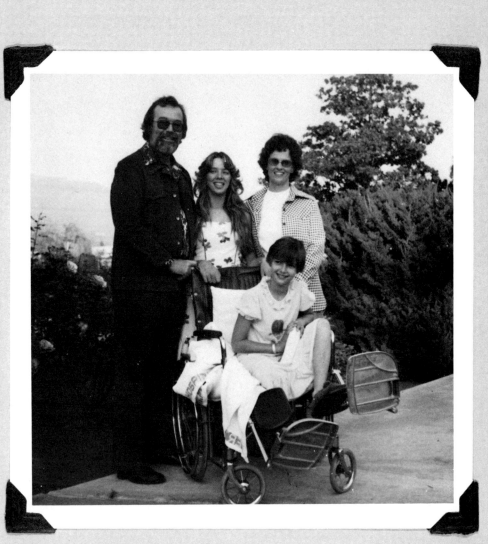

We all look a little tired, but it isn't everyday you lose a leg. At least the surgery is over.

Mom and Dad helped me give my "Chemo-completion" party at the City of Hope to say thank you to everybody and to show i was finished with chemotherapy. We had cake and ice cream...it was great!

Joy Sutera, my favorite nurse came.

And Dr. Rosen too.

Even Dr. Moor came to my party. He drove a long way and brought the letter i sent him after he left the hospital. He keeps it framed over his desk.

Here's the letter, but i goofed. i drew my picture with two legs, but i erased one when i remembered.

Dr. Moor
I Love You
I miss You
♡
Michelle

i looked like a funny Barbie doll with my wooden leg and bald head, but i didn't have to use my crutches. i could hardly wait to show my cousin Jim.

Kim loaned me her hair any time i needed it.

Being bald wasn't so bad!

i got to Take my family to Las Vegas in June 1978. They were there when i got the Victor Award. Wayne Newton presented my award and then surprised me with my very own horse— i named him Prince Wayne Newton.

Wayne Newton is a very special friend to me. He gave me Prince, but best of all he gave me lots of love.

Photo by Donna Kennedy, Press-Enterprise

i tried skiing and loved it so much that before long...

SKIING

MICHELLE
IS ON HER WAY
TO THE
HANDICAPPED
NATIONALS
WINTER PARK . COLORADO

We were on our way to Winter Park, Colorado to compete in the Handicapped National Championships.

Ready or not, here i come!

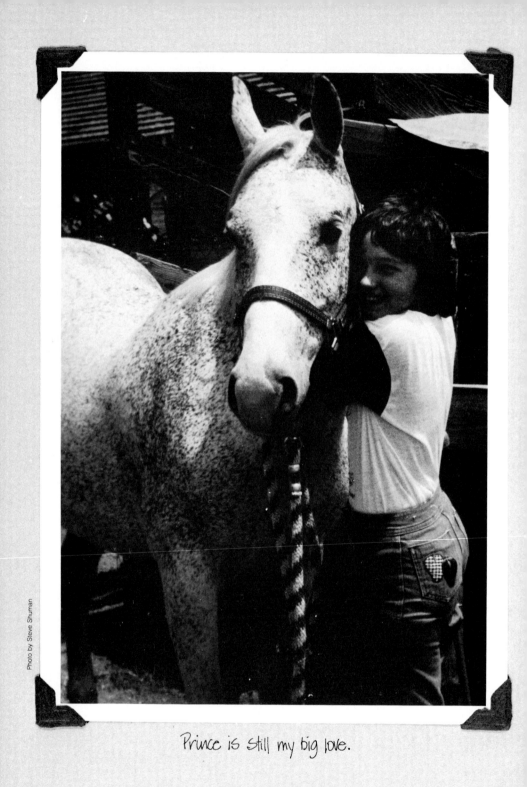

Prince is still my big love.

But having a horse means a lot of hard work. He's gotta have a bath...

and my saddle is really heavy (that's why i let Mom share in some of the "fun").

Training time is important too because we may be going to the 1981 Pentatulon.

Getting up isn't very hard...

He's really special!

As long as Prince doesn't move!

Look hard... can you see my seat belt?

Sometimes i think i could ride forever!

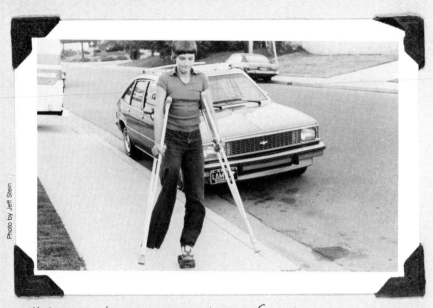

it took a while to get the hang of skating on one leg...

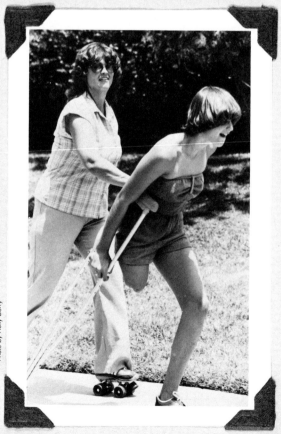

but once i got it down—
LOOK OUT!

Dad wasn't real happy with my approach to sea-sports. I just wanted to give him a lift!

i'll try anything on land !

Tennis is my latest racquet...

and i love it!

Dad wasn't real happy with my approach to sea-sports.
I just wanted to give him a lift!

i'll try anything on land!

Photos by Rick Brubaker

Tennis is my latest racquet...

and i love it!

Take a good look at my family—They're really special!

My life is full of love and promise, and every time the sun goes down i thank God for one more day.

Back cover photo by Tom Kasser

dusted with a powdered sugar topping. A haze hung lightly in the valley making the trees seem like part of a movie setting instead of the living landscape.

"Michelle?" Laura called, approaching her daughter through the slippery snow. "You alright, honey?"

Shelly squealed excitedly, throwing her arms around Laura's waist. "It's so beautiful. Thank you. Thank you for bringing me. I can't believe it."

Looking around, Michelle saw a man walking with a limp and a girl about her age who was also missing a leg. Not far away a red-cheeked, laughing man skied past, the stumps of both legs secured inside boot-like structures clamped to his skis. Everyone seemed so comfortable, so *normal*.

Dick crunched through the snow and stopped beside Michelle, his arm on her shoulder. His nose was red and the breath from his mouth fogged his glasses when he leaned forward to talk to her. "Well, Price, what do you think?"

She looked around her briefly then let out a big puff of warm breath that hung in the air. "I think I'm scared."

To qualify, Michelle had to ski the course for placement in a competition division according to her time and ability level. She was assigned a number to be used for all her statistics this week. Laura helped her work the white bib with its black number 143 over her head and secure it with ties at the sides. Michelle pulled it into place over her parka, tugging clumsily at it with both hands stuffed into her black leather mittens. She smiled broadly while Dick snapped several pictures.

It was mid-afternoon and time for her qualifying run. Michelle and Laura caught the lift to the top. They swung in over the landing area and prepared to get off. Michelle quickly pushed off into the snow and Laura followed suit a little slower. The lift nearly swept her right back down the mountain. Laura made a mental note to improve her speed next time around.

She was laughing, a little embarrassed at her lack of expertise when she caught up to Michelle and was surprised that Michelle had nothing to say. She seldom passed up a good chance to tease her mom. "Honey," Laura questioned as they neared the starting point, "what's wrong?"

Michelle kept her head down, running an outrigger back and forth in the snow making a trail. Finally, without looking up she admitted in a small voice, "I'm so scared." Laura reached for Michelle's arm and they stood facing each other beside a snow-crusted pine.

"Honey, you don't have to do this if you don't want to," Laura reassured her. "You know that, don't you?"

"I know," she said, "but I want to." She paused a minute then looked up at Laura, "I'm just afraid I can't."

"Forget about the time then," Laura suggested pulling the child close to her. "When they call you, ski just for the fun of it."

"Maybe that's what I'll do," she said thoughtfully.

Laura faced her squarely and said gently, "We love you no matter what you do here, Shelly. Do you know that?"

Michelle pulled one arm out of the outrigger and circled her mother's neck. "I'm OK now, Mommy," she said. "I'm just scared, but I really want to try."

"Would it help if I follow you down the hill outside the course?"

Michelle nodded, working her arm and the thick blue sleeve of her parka back into the outrigger grip. She pulled her white knit cap further over her ears and started moving the last few feet into her place in the order of entrants.

The haze was becoming more like a light fog and the air was getting colder. Finally Michelle's number was called. She positioned herself on the platform behind the black and white starting arm. She pushed her outriggers back and forth in the snow, nervously biting her lower lip as she glanced up at the starter. He was a small, round, man with a red hunting cap pulled down over his ears. The big fur collar of his navy blue parka stood up around his neck, half hiding his face. She didn't think he looked very friendly.

She searched the faces on her left until she found Laura's, holding her mother's gaze for a moment, as if making some sort of decision. Then smiling weakly she looked back down the course.

Right below the starting platform there was a steep downgrade where she would pick up quite a bit of speed. Then it seemed to quickly level off and become an easier descent that rounded into a wide turn to the left. She couldn't see the finish line from where she stood but the wind was whipping the plastic triangle flags on the red slalom poles.

Laura studied Michelle's back, wondering whether she should pull her from the race. She knew the child was afraid, but also knew that Michelle would not try something she didn't feel strong enough to do.No, she decided, she'd just wait it out and let Michelle take the lead. If she wanted to go down the hill she was going to have the chance to find out how much she believed in herself.

"143, ready?" the starter asked tersely. She nodded her OK without looking back at him. She preferred not to see him again right now. Her heart was beating rapidly and she could feel the pulsing under her goggles on the sides of her face. She closed her eyes briefly. Her eyeballs felt like they'd frozen solid. Her fingers hurt from being so cold and holding the outriggers so tightly.

"GO!" she heard behind her. Her body tensed up and in that split second she committed herself to going down that hill. Nothing else mattered just then. She was going to give it all she had.

She crouched low and pushed herself off the snow-covered platform with a sharp downward thrust on the outriggers. Her ski left the ground momentarily as she pushed open the black and white barrier and jumped into that first steep grade. She picked up speed and could feel the packed snow bumping by underneath her narrow aluminum ski as she shifted her weight, leaning into the first turn around the flag coming rapidly up in front of her.

Laura stood momentarily frozen at the top of the hill. She was a beginning skier herself and as the full slope came into view in front of her it took her breath away. *These were intermediate slopes?* As she stood there she realized she wasn't sure she *could* ski that hill even if Michelle did need the moral support it would give her.

She looked off to her right and down the hill ahead of her. Michelle was already dipping and moving rhythmically in and out between the flags like a dancer. She watched for a brief moment then decided she was going to have to tackle the hill. She'd promised Michelle, and she had to get down somehow, anyway.

She eased over the summit and into the downhill grade. Michelle was yards ahead of her by now, but Laura was no match for the grade of this slope. She began to zigzag back and forth outside the course markings leaving a razorback trail in the snow. She hoped two things, that Michelle would realize she'd tried, and that somehow she'd end up at the bottom safely. It was going to be a long way back.

Michelle quickly skied out of Laura's sight around the bend in the course by this time and Dick and Kim were standing at the bottom straining to see her blue parka somewhere on the white mountainside. Suddenly, at the top of the course a small figure appeared, slipping easily between the poles on the slalom.

"There she is!" Kim shouted excitedly. "Right at the top!"

"That can't be her," Dick said hoping he was right. "That skier is really traveling. Michelle isn't that fast."

As they watched they realized it was, indeed, Michelle and she was, in fact, traveling down that mountain at a very good clip. Dick snapped several pictures and each time he advanced the film his excitement grew a little more. The closer she got to the finish line the bigger his grin became, until, by the time she slipped through the final markers, he was laughing out loud with pride and amazement.

"She made it!" Kim shouted with cheerleader expertise. "Michelle! You did it! You were great!"

Michelle coasted into the safety area across the finish line as the crowd cheered and beat their gloved hands together in a muffled applause. She stood frozen to her outriggers, her eyes glazed, her expression unchanged. Kim could see from a distance that something was wrong and ran the last few feet to her little sister.

"Michelle? Honey?" Kim called putting her hands on the little girl's shoulders. "Michelle, what's wrong? What is it?"

Suddenly Michelle realized Kim was talking to her. "Oh, Kim!" she cried, throwing her arms, outriggers and all, around her, "I was so scared! I was so *scared!*"

Kim pulled her close and let her cry until she felt the little girl's body relax against her. "It's alright," she said. "Don't worry about it honey. Everything's OK."

"Michelle Price, number 143; time 47.80!" the voice sounded over the loudspeakers.

Dick reached the girls realizing something was wrong. "Are you alright, Michelle?" he asked anxiously. "What's wrong, Kimmy?"

"I think she's OK now, Daddy. She was just scared."

"Honey," he reassured her, "you don't have to compete if it frightens you. This is supposed to be fun for you."

"I'm OK, Daddy," she said, pushing her goggles onto her forehead and rubbing icy cold tears from her face with her mittens. "I was just really scared. But I did it!" She smiled at them sheepishly.

Kim and Dick hugged her soundly and agreed, "You did it!"

"And you made good time, Shelly," Dick added. "Hey! Speaking of time, where's your mother?"

They looked blankly at each other, then Michelle said, "She was going to ski down with me on the outside of the course 'cause I was so scared."

They turned toward the fog-covered mountain, looking for a slow-moving blue and yellow figure. "There she is!" Michelle shouted, pointing about halfway up the hillside. "She's right at the second turn."

Before long Laura slid into the trio waiting for her at the bottom of the hill. No one said a word. They simply looked at each other and burst out laughing, wrapped their arms around one another and headed for the warming house, ravenous and ready for something hot to drink.

As they worked their way through the crowd, another skier joined them, moving next to Michelle. He was a nice looking man with dark hair and a small moustache. His sherwood green parka accented his dark eyes. The pant leg and sleeve on his left side were missing but he moved smoothly down the hill on one ski and an outrigger shoulder extension.

"You were great," he said grinning broadly at Michelle. "How long you been skiing?"

"Not very long," she grinned back liking him instantly, "but I sure love it."

"It shows," he said. "There's nothing like that feeling when you're flying down the mountain, is there?"

"I was pretty scared today; that's a pretty steep course," she admitted. "But sometimes I don't even feel the ground. It's like being a big bird."

"Aren't you Jim Stacy, the actor?" Kim asked recognizing the man skiing with them.

He nodded a little self-consciously, "Yeah, I just wanted to tell this little gal what a great job she did up there."

"Wasn't that something!" Dick said shaking Jim's hand. "We're so proud of her."

"Honey, he never would have guessed that," Laura said teasing

Dick about his enthusiasm. "We're the Prices, Dick and Laura," she said warmly to the smiling young man. "And these are our daughters, Kim, and of course, you know Michelle."

"We're proud of Laura too, though," Dick said. "She made it down the mountain in only 12 minutes, 15 seconds."

Laura blushed a little and poked Dick. Jim was one of the family already, joining in the fun. Accepting him as a welcome member, they shared their meal and a growing friendship.

Competition began early the next day and the Prices eagerly watched the people around them. At the starting gate there waited a young man in his late twenties. On his feet, too small for his body, were walking boots. From the waist up Rene Kirby, was normal, and powerfully developed, but his legs were short, misshapen and all but useless to him. His skis dangled at the ends of his arms with his hands inside the ski boots.

When the starter began his countdown, the young man leaned forward, put his skis to the ground and pushed off with his feet, skiing down the mountain on his hands, his face less than three feet from the snow. The final few feet he raised his legs high in the air and skied across the finish line upside down. The expression on his face belonged to a man who would never be accused of giving up.

Crowds of observers, handicapped and normal, cheered the skiers on, encouraging and supporting each one. The handicapped know what it is to be limited, and somehow they share a knowledge that physical limitations are not the worst ones. With determination and fortitude they push past their limits and onto things normal people fear. They stand squarely and master dragons that corner and control others. In their handicaps many find the real meaning of true freedom.

The women's class "C" division in giant slalom was being run now and Michelle waited again at the starting gate. The morning air was cold and clear and the view from the mountain breathtaking. She took a slow deep breath and threw her head back tasting the sweetness of the air. A flawless blue sky was interrupted here and there with small, white clouds and the sun shone brightly, reflecting brilliantly off the endless white snow.

She watched the starter as he signaled the skier before her to

begin her descent. The woman, a four-tracker skiing with her prosthesis and outriggers, jumped through the wooden starting arm and
down the incline into the course before the starter took his eyes off
her. He seemed to lean as she leaned and feel the snow under the
skier's blades. From where Michelle stood she could see that under
his red hunter's cap were a pair of warm blue eyes. His graying
eyebrows were bushy and matched his thick moustache giving him
an "old fashioned" look, like a character from *The Music Man* or
someone who'd sing in a barbershop quartet on Saturday nights.

The descending skier rounded the turn and could no longer be
seen, so the old man straightened up and walked the few steps back
toward his lean-to. As he looked up he noticed Michelle watching him
and stopped abruptly. He lowered his head slightly, peering out from
under his shaggy eyebrows without blinking for a second or two, then
he curled one side of his mouth up into a large grin.

"You goin' down as fast today as you did before?" he asked her,
resuming his walk and pulling the starting arm across the platform
behind him.

"Did I go down too fast yesterday?" she asked a little surprised he
remembered her.

"First time jitters, I'd guess." He leaned against the wall of the little
shelter checking the time clock before looking back at Michelle. The
numbers were still running, the other skier had not finished her run
yet.

"I was pretty scared," she said shyly. "I haven't skied very long,
just a couple of times since I lost my leg."

"That all?" he said raising his eyebrows and nodding a mute
approval. "You're pretty good then. Just make your start a little
smoother and relax. You should do real well."

He got his signal that the course was clear. It was time for
Michelle. He cleared his timer, "You ready?"

She nodded looking intently down the course, then called back to
him, "Thanks."

"GO!" she heard him say as she pushed through the arm in front
of her. *Smooth he said,* she thought as she pushed into the downhill
slope. She pushed against the knoll and slipped easily down the
grade and into the first turn. *Lean into the turn, that's what Paul said.
Lean and relax. It's such a long way to the bottom.*

She dipped and swayed evenly and gracefully moving in and out between the red and blue gates of the giant slalom, until the fear she'd felt yesterday was far behind her and she moved easily into the thrill of the downhill descent. The cold wind cut against her cheeks and made her eyes feel cold, even behind the goggles. She could hear the blade of her ski cutting through the packed snow underfoot and a spray of snow shot out from under the outriggers as she slid out of one turn, dipping into the next. It felt good to be flying down the mountain. Her leg ached for a rest and her fingers were like long icicles inside her leather mittens but it was worth it. This was the greatest feeling in the world.

"Michelle Price, number 143, time 35.78"

Cheers of approval and excitement came from the people standing around the finish line. Jim Stacy was there with the family. Everyone was thrilled, especially Michelle. She had conquered her fear and skied a good run. She'd grown up a little bit.

They watched the competition the rest of the day and at one point saw a young man descending the hill while a second skier skied opposite him just outside the course.

"How come there's two skiers, Daddy?" Michelle asked as they watched the figures descend the mountain.

"The man on the course is blind," Dick explained. "The other skier is his spotter. He's acting as the man's eyes."

"You mean he tells him what *he* sees?"

"That's right. He's talking to the blind man all the way through the course, telling him where the pontoons are and when to lean to get around them, and things like that." Dick felt his stomach tighten as he thought what it would be like flying down that hill on skis, unable to see where he was going.

"Is that the way a plane lands in the fog?" Michelle asked beginning to understand the teamwork involved.

"A lot like that," Dick answered putting his arm on her shoulder. "You'd really have to trust the person guiding you in either case, wouldn't you?"

"I *guess!*" she said shaking her head. "I don't think I could do it."

The crowd cheered the blind man on enthusiastically. All around them were onlookers fighting back tears, shouting encouragement to the man skiing down the hill toward them. His courage was contageous, inspiring everyone who watched, whether their handicaps were ones that could be seen or those held tightly within.

Competitors at Winter Park understand about *risk*. For them there's risk in simply being alive, in doing the things "normal" people take for granted, like getting to work and fixing meals. At Winter Park people come face to face with a choice we all make every day—to give up or keep on trying.

The entire week went too quickly for everyone. Michelle competed in the slalom and giant slalom and earned two silver medals and a trophy for best overall in her class, presented with great fanfare at the awards banquet the closing night.

As the little white Chinook worked its way through Colorado toward California the next morning, Michelle realized she'd learned much about herself and her world. She learned a lot about conquering fear and discovered she was capable of dreaming great dreams and then working to make some of them come true. She learned that, as she had suspected, we are truly handicapped most cruelly by our own choices. "If you're going to be brave," she quipped, "you've got to do something that scares you."

Winter Park and the National Handicap Championship stand for so much more than ski medals and competition. It is a place where people reach for a greater prize, where they stretch themselves in the trying. The medals symbolize the best times in events. But all the contestants there are winners because of a belief in themselves and a commitment to never give up.

So as the snow falls silently on the ancient fragrant pines, slowly covering the footprints and ski trails weaving their way through the slopes and valley of Winter Park, it cannot disguise what is there. Days spent there are sweet. Friends met there are special. Even time cannot erase the pungent scent of victory in the air.

10
Swept Off Her Foot

Dick settled back against the fat, cool pillow and drew in a deep breath. He smoothed the top of the sheet over the edge of the light green blanket and crossed his arms on his chest.

"It's been a long day," he said wearily to Laura as she sat down on her side of the bed. She lifted her feet off the floor onto the sheets and looked at Dick out of the corner of her eye.

"You look so comfortable," she said in maternal tones. Then gripping the blanket firmly by the hem she yanked the covers off and flung her arm across him before he had a chance to stop her. Dick laughed with surprise, but wasted no time in a counterattack. Employing well developed ability he defended his title of "fastest tickler in the family," until Laura choked out, "Enough."

For a minute or two they both lay panting against their pillows laughing and gasping for air like two high schoolers at a pillow fight. Then Dick circled Laura's waist with his arm. "You're nuts," he said as if convinced it was the truth, "but I love you."

She turned on her side to face him and lightly touched his face. "I'm glad, 'cause I have some neat news and I'd hate to tell it to somebody who didn't love me."

"What news?" he asked picking up the excitement in her voice.

"Well," she grinned, "when I took Michelle to the City of Hope for her treatment today we saw Dr. Rosen."

"And . . ." he persisted.

"And," she said, pausing for effect, "he told me some great news."

"For Pete's sake, Laurie, what'd he say?" He moved his hand toward her throat in mock agitation. "Say it!"

"He said that Michelle is one of the kids they nominated for the Victor Award this year."

"You're kidding!" he said raising his eyebrows and propping himself up on one elbow. "You mean the Sportsmen's Club thing?"

"I guess so," Laura answered. "I'm really not sure about any of the details. But Dr. Rosen was so excited I figured it had to be pretty special."

"Oh, wow," Dick said dropping back on the pillow and looking up at the ceiling. "It's special alright. The Sportsmen's Club does this every year. I never dreamed Michelle . . . ."

"Tell me about it, honey," Laura asked, moving close and resting her head on his shoulder.

He pulled her closer and began to explain, "Every year they choose people from the sports world who've achieved a lot in their area and have acted like winners in other ways too. They've honored people like Roy Campanella, Mark Spitz, Bill Walton . . . ."

"Don't they know any women athletes?"

"What are you, liberated?" he teased. "I was just getting to the women . . . ."

"That's what they all say."

"Just last year they gave one to Kathy McMillan, and before that Sandra Palmer, and Greta Anderson. Chris Evert's been given a Victor too. I think they've been doing this for 10 or 11 years."

"It sounds great," she said smiling slightly. "Just think, our Michelle . . . ."

"The neat part is that she'd hear somebody besides us tell her she's done a great job and been a champ through all this. When are they going to make their final choice?"

"He didn't say," Laura said thinking back over the conversation with Dr. Rosen. "He just said somebody would call in the next week or two to talk to us."

By the end of the week Laura received a phone call setting up an interview time at the house for the whole family. The day arrived and right on schedule the doorbell rang.

"Hi, I'm Rusty Citron," the bearded young man said, smiling and holding out his hand, "and this is Laurie, my assistant. We called—"

"Of course," Dick said opening the door wider, "come on in."

They stepped into the hallway and Rusty eyed a lone cowboy boot standing against the wall.

Following Rusty's glance Dick said, "We can make a pair of shoes last a long time that way. Only wear 'em out one at a time."

Rusty glanced at his partner and they smiled at Dick's easy attitude.

Hearing the voices, Michelle came hopping out of the kitchen and threw her arms around Dick's waist.

"Shelly," Dick said, "this is Rusty Citron and his friend Laurie, from the City of Hope."

"Hi," she said flashing a grin mixed with shyness and fun.

"Hi, Michelle," Laurie said. "We've sure heard a lot about you. I'm glad to finally meet you."

Michelle shrugged self-consciously, quickly asking, "Wanna sit in here?" Before the question was out she was hopping toward the living room. Rusty and Laurie grinned at Dick and Laura and followed the leader.

Laurie was young and her warm eyes were very soft behind the large glasses she wore. Her curly brown hair and easy smile made Michelle relax quickly, answering questions and telling stories like an "old salt."

"Tell me something special that's happened to you this last year, Michelle?" Laurie asked adjusting on her tape recorder.

"Well, there's Lady," Michelle said.

"Lady?" Laurie questioned for more details.

"Yeah, Mommy and Daddy asked what I wanted after my treatments were over. And I told them I wanted a dog, a raccoon and a horse." She reached one hand up and brushed aside a ragged strand of hair. Her chemotherapy treatments had been spaced for every six weeks now, and her hair was growing back in patches, between treatments.

"Well, is Lady your raccoon or what?" Rusty asked teasing Michelle into more conversation.

"Nope, Lady's my dog," she grinned back at the curly-haired man sitting on the couch.

"And what about the raccoon and the horse?" he asked.

"Well, I traded the raccoon in for a different kind of pet. Wanna see him?" she said hopping to a standing position. "He's in the backyard."

"OK," Laurie said shutting off the recorder and taking Michelle's hand.

"Would you hand me my crutch?" Michelle asked her mother.

"What kind of pet did you trade for," Laurie asked, honestly curious.

"Just wait till you see," Michelle grinned, heading at her usual breakneck speed toward the backyard, pulling Laurie by the hand, the other adults in hot pursuit.

"There he is," she said as they stepped into the warm April sunshine. "That's Midnight, my crow." She walked over to a large walk-in cage and opened the screened door. "Come on. Come pet him. He won't bite."

Gingerly Rusty and Laurie followed Michelle into the cage in the middle of the yard and pulled the door shut. Michelle chattered animatedly about the care and feeding of big black crows.

"Don't they look cute," Laura whispered to Dick.

"We should have a picture of them all crowded in that cage," he grinned. "I'm impressed. They're great people."

"And what about the horse, Michelle?" Rusty asked as they stepped back into the cool living room a few minutes later. "Did you ever find a horse?"

"Well, we found a place where we can board one. We can't keep it here 'cause our backyard isn't big enough," she explained. "We just didn't find the right horse yet. But we're looking."

Dick and Laura glanced at each other.

"Can you ride, Michelle?" Laurie asked.

"Of course," she said, matter-of-factly as though every one-legged girl rides horses. "I ride all the time. I get to go over to my friend's house and ride every Monday."

Easy, interesting conversation made the hours pass quickly for everyone.

"You'll be hearing from someone," Rusty said as he and Laurie climbed into his little Toyota. "It was a great afternoon!"

A few days later someone else from the City of Hope paid a visit to the Price's. Sid Keith was warm and friendly as he told the Price family that Michelle had been their final choice to receive the Victor Award for 1977. It took days to call the friends who had prayed so faithfully and share the good news. But it was important to Dick and Laura that those who had so willingly shared in the pain and tears should share in the joy now. The hardest part would be waiting until June when the ceremonies were scheduled in Las Vegas, Nevada. It would seem like forever.

A few days later Kim stood barefoot, dressed in a slip, ironing her dress for work when the phone rang beside her.

"It's Laurie, Mom," she said holding the phone out to Laura. "She wants to talk to you."

"Hi, Laura," the young woman said into the phone. "I've got a kind of odd question to ask you."

"Hardly anything surprises me anymore," Laura said. "What do you need?"

"Good. Then how about this: If we were able to find a horse for Michelle somewhere, would it be alright for her to have one?"

Laura took a deep breath and touched Kim on the shoulder. "Do you really think you could find her a horse?"

Kim's eyes widened as she set the iron down.

"Well, it's a good possibility," Laurie continued, "but we'd have to be sure it was OK with you and Dick before we made any arrangements."

"Oh, yes," Laura said excitedly. "It's just fine with us. That would be so wonderful."

Laura stood with the phone to her ear as Kim hugged her silently, her eyes brimming with tears of joy.

"Well, then," Laurie continued, "there's just one more question. What kind of horse were you looking for?"

"Well, we don't want a rocking horse," Laura said smiling. "Like my mother always says, 'beautiful inside and out.' That's all we care about. It would need to be gentle and good to Michelle—one that would learn to love her as much as she'll love the horse."

"Well, that's a pretty big order. But we'll do our best. Just one more thing, Laura. Can we keep this a secret? In fact, if only you and Dick know that would be best."

"Kim's standing here right now," Laura explained. "But we can make it a secret between us girls. We can even surprise Dick and Rick."

"Sounds like fun to me," Laurie said laughing. "We'll be getting back in touch soon."

For the next few weeks Kim and Laura had a wonderful time keeping their secret. There were times it was hard not to say something but the thought of everyone's delight at the presentation kept them going.

Finally the day came when they were to fly to Las Vegas and early morning found the household in a colorful uproar.

"Michelle," Kim hollered down the hall. "Where's the hair-dryer?"

"I packed it already," she yelled back from her room. "You don't expect me to get my award looking like a scarecrow do you? I have to be beautiful."

Kim left her room long enough to throw a pillow at Michelle who flopped "wounded" on her bed beside her open suitcase.

Before long they were all settled aboard the big yellow Hughes Airwest. The plane trembled as the pilot revved up the engines for takeoff from the California airport. Michelle pressed her nose against the window and watched the runway roll by faster and faster until she was forced back against the seat when the tail of the plane dipped low. She rested her head against the high seatback and smiled slightly listening to the high-pitched hum of the engines. Looking out the window again she could see miniature houses and cars, even tiny little people walking the ribbonlike streets below, so far away.

"It's like dreaming," she said quietly.

"What'd you say, honey?" Rick asked, touching her shoulder as she sat watching the world below her.

"It's like dreaming," she repeated. "Everything looks like somebody painted it. It doesn't even look real."

In what seemed like no time, the Las Vegas airport came into view, and they were in rapid descent over the city.

After they landed the hostess pulled the big door open and a warm breeze pushed into the plane. Michelle grabbed her blue denim cap to keep the wind from snatching it off her head as she started down the stairs, briefly watching a snub-nosed yellow cart with two empty trailers roll under the belly of the plane.

"What's that for?" she yelled back up the stairs to Kim.

"I think that's how they bring the suitcases into the airport," Kim answered, closing the gap between them.

They picked up their luggage and loaded it into a big white limousine the Victor Awards committee arranged for them. With eyes the size of quarters Michelle pronounced it "a block long" as it carried the family smoothly over the desert streets and onto the crowded and flashy Las Vegas Strip.

Finally they made the turn into the drive of the Hilton Hotel. "Is this *our* hotel?" Michelle asked, pressing her cheek and nose against the window straining to see the top.

"Well, we're going to stay here for the next couple of days," Dick teased, "but it's not really ours."

The valet at the entry opened the door for them and Michelle hopped onto the sidewalk. Her face reflected the excitement of what she saw around her. The rest of the family, seeing things through her enthusiasm found that they agreed, this was pretty exciting any way you looked at it.

Pushing through the revolving door, Laura stepped into the lobby and turned to watch Michelle's reaction to the splendor and noise of the Las Vegas crowds just inside.

Michelle pushed the big brass door through its casing and, as if she'd just finished her turn at jump rope, hopped through the opening into the carved marble and brass lobby. Rich colors and ornate styling were everywhere as she stood just inside the entrance looking all around, and overhead.

Her eyes widened as she worked her way to the edge of the lobby, peering fascinated into the noisy casino and the sea of people a few steps below her. The ratchety sound of slot machines and ringing "jackpot" bells played a staccato background for the cheering of people at the playing tables or under the flashing signals of yielding slots. The unmistakable sound of silver dollars falling into hollow metal trays seemed continuous. Everywhere she looked there were people—dressed in shorts and bathing suit tops, evening gowns or tuxedos with the shirts unbuttoned and bow ties clipped to one side of the collar.

"What do you think?" Laura asked her, moving to the railing on the edge of the casino.

"Boy, look at this place!" Michelle said almost in a whisper. "Are we really going to stay here?"

"If I get us checked in we are," Dick said, walking up and patting her shoulder. "Want to help?"

Stepping up to the carved marble registration desk Dick smiled pleasantly at the uniformed man on the other side. "You have a reservation," he said evenly, "for Dick Price."

Nodding professionally the man moved to a rack beside his station and sorted through several slips of paper stacked in a slot marked "P-Q-R." He shuffled through them a second time, replaced them and returned to the window. "I'm sorry, sir. There is no reservation for a Dick Price."

Dick blinked, raised his eyebrows and asked, "How about Richard Price? Or R.C.?"

The man simply shook his head.

Dick looked puzzled as he turned to Laura and Kim beside him. "Would it be under Michelle's name, Daddy?" Kim asked as a wild guess.

"Oh, Michelle Price," the man behind the desk echoed pleasantly. "I have a reservation for a Michelle Price."

Michelle grinned broadly and threw her chin up in a pose she hoped looked important. Somehow her wooden crutch, one leg and ragged hairdo didn't match the face she made, and everyone including the hotel clerk burst into laughter.

"Michelle," the man said leaning across the counter to see his small patron better, "this is your credit card for your stay with us. Everything is in your name, so you'll have to buy dinner for the family and you'll be the one to pay for the room. It's your treat this time."

"OK!" she said grinning. "I like that idea."

"Well, you can start by signing the register for me if you will," he said smiling back.

The rooms were bright and cheerful, decorated in wood tones and a restful shade of green. Michelle staked "first dibs" on the elegant marble bathroom, claiming a desperate need for a leisurely bath. Before long everyone was freshened up and ready to tackle the penthouse reception for Victor recipients and celebrities. It was scheduled for 5 P.M.

As they stood waiting for the elevator to take them to the top of the Hilton Hotel, Laura made a silent last-minute check of everyone. They all looked wonderful—and excited. She noticed a warm sensation within her as she silently thanked the Lord for His goodness to them, all of them, in honoring Michelle as a Victor. "Let it all count for you, Lord," she whispered as the elevator doors slid open and they filed inside.

Michelle wore a long blue and white peasant dress and stood beside her brother looking straight ahead, discreetly poking her elbow into his ribs every chance she got. Rick said as the car came to a stop, "Just you wait, Price, I'll get you." She landed one last subtle jab as the doors slid open.

The carpeting was a deep peacock blue and seemed to swallow their feet as they stepped into it in the entrance. For a brief moment they just stood taking it all in. No one spoke. Chandeliers sparkled brightly, illuminating the well-dressed, attractive people scattered in pairs and small groups around the room.

People filled the large room, milling, talking, moving slowly around the floor, sitting at small tables, leaning against an ornate railing or the forest green walls.

Barely in the room they heard a friendly voice call out, "Michelle, I'm so glad you're here."

Laurie walked briskly toward them, smiling, her long powder-blue skirt flowing softly around her ankles.

"It's nice to see someone we know," Laura said, hugging Laurie warmly.

"I'll say," Dick said, taking her outstretched hand. "Are we late?"

"Not at all," Laurie assured them. "Come over here and let's get you something to eat."

As they worked their way toward the long white table against the wall they noticed Tom Bosley of "Happy Days" fame talking with a tall gray-haired man with bushy eyebrows. Not far away Marion Ross spoke pleasantly with Rusty Citron and a young girl in her late teens. Rusty looked up and waved as Laurie led the Prices through the room.

At a small table in the center of the room Paul Williams and Alice Cooper talked energetically over small plates of food. And as they zigzagged through the room they passed Dr. "J", Tommy John and Chris Evert.

Suddenly they stood before an enormous table, its clean white linen cloths nearly hidden by a harvest of culinary creations. In the center stood a three-foot ice statue of a thrashing fish poised gracefully erect on its tail, jaws open. Up and down the table were carved-ice clam shells, opened wide, housing hors d'oeuvres of many kinds: clam creations, crabmeat in exotic sauces and vegetables prepared for unlimited enjoyment. Mouth-watering pastries in every shape and flavor imaginable covered gleaming silver trays. Special breads and fancy meats and cheeses seemed to have no end.

Laurie stopped them every now and then to introduce them to different people; Gene and Joyce Klein, the owners of the San Diego Chargers football team; Barron Hilton, president of the Hilton Hotel chain, and others who had turned out for the excitement of the annual Victor Awards.

They settled around a table near the center of the room, and Laurie asked, "How would you like to catch the Wayne Newton Show tonight, Michelle? We've arranged four tickets for you." Michelle looked up and popped a green olive into her mouth, then looked at her mom and dad.

"Sounds wonderful," Dick said.

"That's really a nice extra," Laura said. "I understand his shows are almost impossible to get tickets for."

"You're absolutely right," Laurie said nodding. "He never plays to an empty seat."

"Then the advertising is true?" Dick asked. "He really is Las Vegas's 'Midnight Idol'?"

"He really is," she said grinning. "Wayne Newton is a remarkable performer. He very seldom releases an album and you'll hardly ever see him on TV, but his shows are sold out here, sometimes weeks in advance. He performs more often in Las Vegas than any other entertainer does and he handles just about everything for his shows himself. He chooses the songs he's doing, picks the arrangements; even had the bandstand and stage floor in one of the hotels built to his specifications. He says he loves to perform. Even said he'd probably sing on the street corner if no one paid him to do his shows. I've seen his show a couple of times and I'm crazy about the guy."

"We sure like his music," Laura said. "It would be fun to see him in person."

"Well, good," Laurie said, choosing a piece of carrot off her plate. "Then it's settled. The dinner show, tonight at eight."

Before they left the reception, Laura found Rusty and discreetly asked whether there had been any news on the horse.

"Haven't heard a thing yet," he said shrugging his shoulders. "We just don't know."

Later that night, after finally locating the Wayne Newton tickets (in Michelle's name), they were ushered into a dazzling showroom and shown to a table at the stage.

"When she said tickets," Kim quipped, "I didn't think we'd end up on stage with him."

"These are what you call good seats," Dick said. "Enjoy it. You'll probably never sit here again." They laughed appreciatively and opened the menus.

The stage was concealed behind scarlet velvet curtains, and sparkling chandeliers suspended around the room cast gold and blue hues on the walls and ceiling. They enjoyed their dinner and were talking among themselves when the house lights began to dim and a voice over the loudspeaker said, "Ladies and gentlemen, the Copa Room is proud to present—Mr. Wayne Newton!"

Suddenly an orchestra was playing and the scarlet curtains parted and drew back as the pleasant strains of a man's voice sang out over the applause. From around the still swaying curtain appeared a tall, handsome young man in his mid-thirties in a white suit and red shirt opened at the neck. His deep tan and dark hair added to the brilliance of his smile as he musically greeted his audience, moving easily across the stage looking into their faces. He caught Michelle's eye and his face lit up with a special warmth. He smiled and winked in her direction as he concluded his opening number.

Michelle sat at the very edge of the stage and leaned both elbows on the wooden ledge. Her blue and white dress fell in soft folds onto the plush red carpeting completely camouflaging her "little leg" beneath the skirt. The only outward evidence of illness was the thin, shaggy hair that sparsely covered her head. She watched Wayne Newton intently as he moved through his first number, and enthusiastically banged her hands together showing her approval when the music stopped.

"I thought this show was going to be boring," she yelled across the table to Laura over the applause filling the room.

"How come?" Laura asked in the din.

"I thought he was going to sing old fuddy-duddy music like Daddy listens to," she grinned at Dick. They laughed heartily as the music began signaling another song. She quickly returned her attention to the stage as Wayne Newton lowered his eyes to change the mood. Shelly's brown eyes were clear and dancing with excitement as he slowly raised the microphone and sang softly:

"You are so beautiful to me . . ."

He moved smoothly across the stage in their direction smiling and singing to Michelle. She looked back, barely blinking for fear she might miss something. He walked directly up to her and knelt on one knee as he continued:

"You are so beautiful to me . . ."

He took her hand in his and she just as quickly placed her other hand on top of his, looking intently back into his eyes. She mouthed every word as he sang it and in the middle of the next phrase he looked briefly away to compose himself. Her eyes and attention unnerved him, and he struggled not to laugh out loud.

"You're everything I hoped for, you're everything I need You are so beautiful to me."

His delight showed on his face as he looked at the happy little girl in front of him. The audience applauded the song and his gesture of kindness, but no one enjoyed it more than he and Michelle. He bent down and kissed her lightly on the cheek.

The rest of the show revealed Wayne Newton as a multi-talented person, playing a number of instruments and singing an expansive variety of songs. In the final portion of his show he came on stage wearing a black, three-piece suit, a white shirt and scarf and an enormous turquoise and silver belt buckle. As onlookers applauded his song he loosened the white scarf and walked back to Michelle. Bending down on one knee he draped the scarf over her head. "This is for you, Sweetheart," he said as he winked and smiled at her, then returned center stage to close the show.

As Laura tucked her into bed that night Michelle raised up on one elbow and straightened the scarf beside her on the bed table one last time. "He was awful nice to me," she said kissing her mother goodnight. "I wish I could see him again. He just swept me off my foot!"

11
Royal Answers

Walking into the Hilton Hotel's Green Room Michelle looked around at the people already there. "There's LeVar Burton," she said, hopping off happily to chat with her new friend. She seemed to be at home with people from any walk of life, never stopping to wonder whether she was welcome. She just loved everyone no matter who they were and figured they loved her just the same way. Dick and Laura looked at each other and smiled.

Rick walked toward them with Kim and Brenda. Dick saw them coming and let out a low whistle. "You guys look terrific!" he said sincerely. "You going somewhere?"

"Thanks, Dad," Kim retorted patting his tummy under his cummerbund. "You look pretty good yourself in your ruffled shirt and tux. I've never seen you so dressed up."

"That's because the only other time I wore one of these things was for my own wedding, and you hadn't even been thought of then."

Laura watched the family banter, enjoying the closeness, happy in the warmth of the evening they were here to share. She still pinched herself every now and then making sure it was for real. But tonight was the night Michelle would receive her Victor Award.

A few minutes later the double doors into the Green Room swung open again and Wayne Newton and his aide, Bear, slipped in unnoticed. Wayne stopped just inside the door and watched Michelle for a few minutes as she animatedly crutched from person to person talking freely with everyone. She spent a little time with LeVar Burton enjoying his questions and teasing, and smiled broadly when pictures were taken. She retrieved autographs and conversation from Pat Harrington, Jr., Valerie Bertinelli, Liberace, Foster Brooks and several other stars. She talked with Marion Ross like an old, dear friend.

"She's really something else," Wayne Newton commented to Bear. "Look at her. She's getting around better on one leg than most people do on two."

"She's got the moves, alright," Bear commented grinning widely, his dark skin showing off his white teeth.

"You know," Wayne said, crossing his arms and shifting his weight, "there's something about her. . . . Maybe it's the way she doesn't seem to feel sorry for herself. She really gets to me. When she sat grinning up at me last night at the show, I told Elaine it was love at first sight."

Just about then Michelle looked up and caught a glimpse of Wayne Newton standing in the back of the room. "Wayne Newton," she said loudly as she bounded toward him as fast as she could go. "Hi!" she said brightly, "I didn't know you were going to be here tonight. I really liked your show last night," she said breathlessly.

Wayne Newton entered enthusiastically into the conversation and the friendship, enjoying himself nearly as much as she was, while Bear stood with an amused expression on his face listening to her rattle on beside them.

"Thank you for the scarf. I tied it onto my crutch for tonight, see?" she said, lifting her crutch into the air for him to see.

"That's really nice, Michelle, I'm glad you like it," he said smiling proudly. "I sure enjoyed having you at the show."

"When I grow up I want to do what you do," she said. "I want to be a singer too, only a lady." She opened her eyes wide and laughing a little she asked, "Wanna sit down?" Plopping into a nearby booth she straightened her pink headscarf.

"I'd love to but I can't," he said in confidential tones. "I think I'd tear my pants if I did." They enjoyed the laugh.

"What's your name?" Michelle asked the strapping black man with Wayne Newton.

"I'm called Bear," he said smiling at her.

"Is that your real name?" she asked with interest.

"That's my real name," he said nodding for reinforcement. "My momma named me after a bear she saw before I was born."

"It couldn't have been a polar bear," Wayne said grinning widely.

"Nope," Bear said enjoying the joke. "It was a big, black grizzly." The three of them laughed heartily.

"Wayne," she asked hesitantly, "are you going to give me my award tonight?"

"No, honey," he said slowly. "I'm here to give someone else their award."

Michelle had so hoped he would say yes that his answer took her completely by surprise. Suddenly she found herself choking back tears. "I gotta go now," Michelle said quickly as she swung to her foot and moved rapidly toward the doors and into the hallway.

"She alright?" Wayne asked Kim genuinely concerned.

"She'll be fine," Kim responded smiling. "I'm sure she's OK. I'll check on her in a minute."

Wayne Newton was surprised how quickly he had come to love this little girl. It wasn't hard, because she was a giver he decided, not a taker. She spent her time giving to those around her, helping them to feel better, making them happy. And in the process she found her own happiness.

"If only more people could be like that little girl," he said reflectively as he and Bear walked across the thick carpet to the dressing rooms. He added thoughtfully, "I wish everyone could meet her. She's the epitome of what we all need to know. She portrays a special kind of hope in the dreams she's got. The world needs the kind of hope Michelle gives."

Out in the hall Michelle paced rapidly working off her frustration. She felt silly being so disappointed over such a silly thing, but Wayne Newton had become a special person in her life and somehow she wanted to share this special award with him.

Kim pushed the double doors open quietly and just watched Michelle for a minute. Finally she asked, "You OK, kiddo?"

Michelle looked up at Kim, stopped pacing and took a deep breath. "Silly, huh?" she said hanging her head.

Kim put her arm around her little sister as they walked back into the Green Room, "I'd never call it silly. This is a pretty important night for you. And I'm proud of you, Michelle." They stopped in the aisle as the doors swung shut behind them and hugged each other soundly.

Finally the showroom at the Las Vegas Hilton was filled to capacity and the Twelfth Annual Victor Awards were under way. The stage was a myriad of lights and rainbows, and at the plexiglas podium a handsome young man who looked like he'd stepped off the list of Best Dressed Men stood waiting for the music and applause to die down. His tuxedo accented his ebony coloring and broad shoulders.

"That's LeVar Burton," Michelle whispered to Kim, proud that she knew his name, happier still that they'd spent some time together.

Celebrities were introduced and they in turn introduced the honored athletes: Rod Carew, baseball; "Dr. J" Julius Erving, basketball; Walter Payton, football; Nancy Lopez, women's golf; Chris Evert, women's tennis; Alberto Juantorena and Francie Larrieu, track and field; and Tommy John, Come Back Athlete of the Year, and many others. Then came a special spot.

LeVar Burton stepped back to the podium and the audience heard him say, "Now we'd like for you to hear a very special story about another kind of inspiring courage. It's about a little girl who's going to be 10 years old next week."

Backstage the cues were given to send Laura, Dick and the family onstage. Laura kissed Michelle lightly on the cheek and whispered, "We'll be praying." Then she lifted her white chiffon skirt and walked up the stairs to the stage with the rest of the family. Michelle went as far as her companion, Jill, would let her, and watched until the family was out of sight.

"Let's fix your sash, honey," Jill whispered hoarsely, "turn around here."

Jill's headset picked up the words of LeVar Burton as he continued, "She was eight years old when she found out she had a malignant bone tumor that was going to cost her a leg. Now, upon hearing this news, most people would have gone into a severe depression. But Michelle Price is no ordinary little girl."

As he spoke he looked out into the audience. Expensively dressed, influential people from all over the country listened intently as he continued. "Her understanding of what was happening to her and the way she handled it is awe-inspiring, and is a great example of what the City of Hope is all about.

"The story should first be told by Michelle's parents, Dick and Laura Price, and their two older children, Kim and Rick who are right here with Wayne."

The cameras picked up Wayne Newton standing with a hand mike beside the Price family. He was pleased to be a part of Michelle's award.

Smiling sincerely, he introduced the Prices to the audience in his resonant voice, "There are questions I'd like to ask you that we've all been wondering about. Dick, when did you first learn of your daughter's illness?"

"We learned of it in November of '76," Dick answered slowly, conscious of the people sitting beyond the lights in the huge hotel showroom.

"And what prompted you to go to the City of Hope?"

"Well," Dick continued, shifting his weight from one foot to the other, and relaxing a little, "we checked many places, about what kind of treatment she would be receiving. We found that the City of Hope reflected what we expected out of a medical institution."

Wayne talked with Dick about Michelle's treatment at the City of Hope bringing out the fact that it is a non-billing institution. As he moved a little closer to Laura the lights glinted off the golden Victor Award he held in his hand. With a tone of understanding coming through his expression Wayne Newton asked Laura, "How did Michelle handle seeing her friends when she came back from the hospital for the first time, if you don't mind my asking?"

"It was hard on her," Laura said softly, remembering the first few days back home. "She was playing with the kids across the street and she knew it was hard on them. So she went to her father and asked if he'd like to take a walk with her. She went door to door and told everyone what had happened to her to put them at ease.

"When she came around to the last house," Laura added, "Michelle said, 'I'm glad it's all over. I think they'll feel a lot better about it.' "

The audience spontaneously applauded expressing their feelings about what Michelle had taken on herself to do.

Wayne's next words were drowned out. When he was able to be heard, Wayne Newton asked Dick, "Have you any advice that you'd like to give parents that might be faced with similar situations?"

Dick briefly looked away then answered, "All I can say is that you can't let fear overcome you. You have to live each day and make the most out of every minute by living on a day-to-day basis." He shifted his weight again and looked out at the audience, his voice filled the room, "And you have to have a lot of faith. Not just in the medical staff, but I believe faith in God helps out too."

The audience applauded their agreement and respect as Wayne Newton laid his hand on Dick's shoulder, "It certainly does," he responded, then turned to the audience and said, "Ladies and Gentlemen, I'd like us all to meet an incredible young lady, Michelle Price!"

Behind him on the stage the rhythmic fountain waters shot their salute into the air as they joyously danced. The orchestra began playing "Michelle" and hearty applause filled the air as the audience strained to see the little girl they wanted so much to meet.

Backstage Jill received her cue and excitedly walked Michelle to the short stairway up to the stage. "Good luck, honey," she said with tears glistening in her eyes.

"Thanks," Michelle shot back earnestly to the young lady urging her on. She stood catching her breath at the foot of the stair when a man with a headset loudly whispered, "Get out there!" The audience was still applauding.

Grabbing her skirt in her hand and hiking it up to her knee she hopped up the step, balanced herself with her crutches and tackled the next step, until she was standing breathless at the top. She dropped her skirt and swung herself forward into the entrance to the stage. As she approached the edge of the open curtain she could hear the wild applause from the audience and felt the warmth from the bright lights cover her arms and face.

Dick and Laura, Kim and Rick turned slightly to see her make her entrance and smiled proudly back at her in her moment of victory. "There she is," Wayne Newton said. His voice was a mixture of pride and tenderness.

She looked like a delicate Dresden doll, her dress a pale pink covered with a gossamer flocking of wildflowers, the organdy sailor bib trimmed in lace, and a matching scarf tied around her head. At the bottom of her long skirt one shiny white shoe swung with her to the mark where she would turn in front of the fountains to walk down the steps and join the family and her new friend.

The already thunderous applause became louder and there were tears in the eyes of the audience. Michelle hesitated at the top of the stage stairway and smiled warmly at her family. She looked radiant, her skin pink, her cheeks rosy, her eyes clear and sparkling. Before descending the stair to the stage floor she smiled at Wayne Newton. He winked back at her.

"You tricked me," she mouthed to him, delighted that he was a part of her big moment.

Dick watched his daughter as she worked her way proudly down the stage stairway under the hot lights. In front of hundreds of people in the showroom and thousands more in the TV audience, she stood tall and held her head high. He thought about her dream to be Miss America and smiled through his tears, *Honey, you're a queen tonight. Your dream is coming true.*

As she rhythmically made her way across the last few feet of stage to Dick and Laura she was almost unaware that the audience was enthusiastically welcoming her and that people all over the room were standing to their feet. The little girl, smiling warmly at everyone around her, touched the hearts of all who watched. Everywhere people were in tears.

Wayne smiled a special smile at his little friend and teased privately, "You thought I was leaving, huh?" The audience's applause began to die.

"Let me ask you a question," Wayne Newton said crouching down on one knee beside Michelle. His voice was full of special secrets as he spoke to this child he'd come to love and respect in the past two days. "Michelle," he asked, "what did you tell the other kids about your leg?"

"Well," she began, opening her eyes wide and tilting her head back slightly, remembering, "sometimes I'd tell them about . . ." She took a deep breath, "Sometimes I would say, I was on a river trip and I fell off the boat and an alligator bit it off, and I got so scared that my hair fell out."

The room immediately filled with a warm, natural laughter.

Michelle and Wayne talked briefly of other interests, then he opened the subject of skiing.

"I hear you're an accomplished athlete, and you like to ski," he began. The bright lights flashed on the award he still held as he moved the hand mike to Michelle for her answer.

With the microphone under her chin she only nodded yes. Her silence tickled Wayne Newton and he looked away briefly collecting himself before pursuing the questioning further. "Was it difficult for you to learn to ski again after your operation?"

He switched the mike back to her again and she looked at it, then self-consciously answered, "Kind of." She looked a little embarrassed as she glanced back at Dick and Laura behind her. They nodded encouragingly and she added, "It was kind of hard, I guess."

"Have you been in any competition since then?" Wayne persisted.

She hesitated, looking at him, "Yeah. I went on the Olympic . . . something." She squirmed slightly, unable to get all the words in the right order, "I forgot what it was called . . ." then remembering part of it, quickly added "the slalom." Her head bobbed up and down as she nodded confirmation of the term.

Obviously amused at her reluctance to tell about her victories on the slopes Wayne Newton continued, grinning broadly, "How well did you do?" The audience was enjoying his difficulty in getting her to tell what he wanted them to know. A muted sound of amusement rose from the attentive audience as they waited.

Dick prompted Michelle quietly from behind and she self-consciously added, "Um, two silver medals." Wayne Newton laughed, the secret finally dislodged. The room filled with a spontaneous applause and the faces around her were smiling encouragement as Wayne Newton presented Michelle with her Victor Award for 1977. They talked about her birthday coming up and the special party she was planning that week to say thank you to everyone at the City of Hope.

"Now," he said, with a sly look, "I happen to know that you love skiing, but it's really not your favorite sport. You want to tell us about your first love?"

"It's horses," she said eagerly. "I love horses."

"How often do you ride?" he asked.

"Every Monday."

"And do you have your own horse?" he prodded.

"No."

"Is there a horse in the future for you?"

"Yeah," she said almost forgetting about the audience and directing her full attention to Wayne, "we're looking for one."

He pulled the mike close to his chin and said almost confidentially, "Can I ask you a question, Michelle? What does the City of Hope mean to you?"

She looked into his dark eyes and said evenly, "Love and faith."

Over the spontaneous applause he commented, "I don't think it could be said any better."

"Tonight, Michelle," he continued, "we've been presenting Victor Awards to athletes who've demonstrated outstanding achievements, and you're one of them. We think extraordinary courage is what you've shown in your fight against one of life's toughest opponents, and that qualifies you to win that miniature Victor you're holding. And we hope you'll enjoy it always, 'cause you're an incredible lady."

Again the audience was on its feet loudly applauding the little girl who'd walked into their hearts just a few minutes before.

"I also know," Wayne Newton said taking a letter from his pocket, and looking at Michelle, "that your favorite star . . . up until last night . . . ?"

They looked at each other, sharing a private joke and Michelle rolled her eyes a little embarrassed, "It's you," she said laughing.

"It's me?" he questioned in mock surprise. Then turning to the audience he explained, "Up until last night her favorite star was Henry Winkler, right, Michelle?" She nodded. Then teasingly he added, "Notice how we changed that around real quick?" They joined in the joke as he opened the letter in his hand.

With her enthusiastic approval he began, "Dear Michelle, first of all, hugs and kisses to you. Last year I spoke to you after you came home from the hospital. This year you're receiving the Special Victor Award in Las Vegas. You must be very proud of yourself, and I'm very proud of you. It is with great regret that I cannot be there with you, but unfortunately, time is not as friendly to me as it once was, and my schedule would not permit my being with you on your special day. Just know, Michelle, that in my heart I'm celebrating your award. Be very good to yourself, and remember, self-respect is joy, and indeed, cool. Love and more love, Henry Winkler."

The audience applauded Henry Winkler's letter and Wayne said, "Now, Michelle, with this Special Victor Award and your tenth birthday coming up this weekend, I went to my ranch and brought along a special gift for you. OK?" he said building the suspense just a little. "I figured if it's personal to me and something I love, you might enjoy it too. I just hope it fits."

Purposely diverting Michelle's attention, he looked over her head and motioned to someone offstage "Uh, if I could get someone to bring it out here." Michelle turned around, straining to see what he was looking at.

Behind her Wayne Newton's trainer appeared leading a regal, cream-colored Arabian gelding. Almost as one body the audience stood, applauding wildly.

Hearing the applause Michelle turned around to see what had happened. There, in front of her stood the biggest, most beautiful horse she'd ever seen. She stared in disbelief, her mouth open as she drew a quick breath and tried to decide whether she could let herself believe what her eyes saw. Could it really be true?

She looked up at Wayne, her face glowing with the joy and ecstasy of Christmas morning. Her eyes were filled with the need for confirmation, assurance that this was not a dream. Wayne stepped beside her and put his hand on her shoulder, nodding the reassurance she sought from him. His eyes brimmed with tears. She looked back at the animal standing like royalty before her and tears filled her eyes. Slowly she leaned forward on her crutches, making her way toward the horse, her shoulders shaking with a trembling joy that pushed out from within her.

"His name is Prince," Wayne said as she crossed in front of him moving toward the animal. His voice cracked. He could not hide his tears.

Standing beside the horse she had prayed for, Michelle reached out her hand and felt Prince's warm breath and velvet muzzle. She seemed almost afraid to touch him, as if it might make him disappear. The trainer held the big animal steady watching the little girl's face. What he saw was all the delight and pure joy anyone could express.

In her eyes danced the dreams and hopes of her young heart. Something deep inside stirred his father-heart and he felt the unbridled joy of the child beside him as she laughed and cried in wonder. The trainer turned his face away from the camera.

The enraptured audience, from every possible walk of life, stood pounding their hands together, tears spilling down their faces—men, women, cameramen, stagehands, celebrities, other Victor recipients, even their tuxedoed host, Wayne Newton. They had been touched by a youngster they would never forget.

Michelle seemed unaware of all of them as she moved slowly toward the horse—her horse. Her eyes danced as she touched Prince again. God works miracles of all kinds. Her prayer had been answered.

12
After the Victor Award

A handsome celebrity on one knee opposite a tired but
beautiful little soldier with one leg—
It was a meeting anointed with honesty and truth:
    a child, simply accepting the star's brilliance
    without pretense,
    a man, with tears in his eyes, reflecting on his
    many blessings—excluding fame.
And eternal love is born between two deserving people.

From a poem written for Michelle
by Ken Millett, October 10, 1979

When she'd finally settled in again at home, Michelle turned her
attention to getting things ready for the chemo-completion party she
would be giving soon. She had one last week of treatment at the City
of Hope, and on the last day they would have the biggest party she
could dream up.

When they left for the hospital everything was ready. "Are you
sure you ordered the cake with a rose garden and a waterfall on it?"
Michelle asked, double-checking as they pulled into the familiar
hospital parking lot.

"I'm sure, honey," Laura smiled patiently, reassuring her for the
fourth time that day.

"And pink punch and balloons?"

"Everything. You saw the bags of stuff in the hallway."

"Yeah," Michelle said, leaning back against the seat thoughtfully. "I just want everything to be really special. It's important. I want it to be nice for my friends."

"It will be, Price," Dick said scooping her off the seat and tucking her under one arm like a sack of potatoes. "You have worked so hard on this you can't miss."

Michelle giggled and flailed around in pretend struggle. She wished it were next week already. She'd much rather be going to the party today instead of into the hospital for more chemotherapy. But this was to be the last time. What a wonderful thought! No more chemotherapy. Never, never again!

"Kaylene," Michelle squealed excitedly. "Hi!"

The small blonde girl smiled broadly, just a little embarrassed by Michelle's noisy exuberance. "Hi!" she called back slipping off her bed and into the hallway beside Michelle's wheelchair. "I didn't know you were going to be here this time."

"Me either. Isn't it neat?!" Michelle reached up and took Kaylene's hand. They were comfortable with each other now. They'd seen each other through the months whenever they'd been admitted together and had built a warm and healthy friendship.

"I'm having a party after my treatment this time," Michelle said excitedly. "Can you come? It's for my friends. It's going to be Friday."

"I don't know," Kaylene said, "but I'll ask. I like parties."

"We're going to have rose garden cake and pink punch and balloons and everything."

"Oh," Kaylene said, eyes sparkling, "it sounds so neat."

Before many days had passed the girls were feeling better and were spending as much time together as possible. Sitting across from Kaylene at the white pedestal table in the playroom, Michelle reached across the red and black playing board to move her checker.

"King me," she said happily. "Now I can chase you all over the board."

"Not if I'm chasing you," Kaylene grinned moving her king after one of Michelle's playing pieces.

"I wonder what's taking our moms so long," Michelle said studying the checkerboard, deciding strategy for her next move.

"Maybe somebody caught them and made them take it back."

They looked at each other, wondering whether they should be afraid.

"Nobody would make them take it back. They don't let you return stuff like that," Michelle said with hopeful authority.

"Boy," Kaylene said, jumping another one of Michelle's men, "I sure hope you're right."

"Me too," Michelle agreed. "I'll bet our mothers got talking and forgot to come back. They sure do like to talk."

Finally the playroom door opened and in walked Laura and Dottie Hall carrying two small packages. Laura peeked down the hall in both directions, then closed the door quietly behind her, tiptoeing toward Michelle and Kaylene. Both girls put their hands over their mouths stifling giggles. Dottie pulled her sweater around her package hiding it from view, pretending to check for intruders behind chairs and drapes.

The parcels were set on the table and carefully opened as the powerful aroma of Italian spices filled the air and Laura and Dottie pulled their chairs up to the girls' table to split their pizzas.

Morning dawned with blue skies and warm sun as though specially ordered for the party. And Michelle was awake before the birds.

When her breakfast tray arrived she was sitting on the edge of her bed, washed, brushed and wearing the new dress Kim had made for the occasion, her first short dress since the surgery.

Her stomach was fluttery but she knew it was just butterflies. The chapter on chemotherapy had been closed and she was doing her best to forget it. Today marked a new beginning and pronounced an end to many painful and frightening days in her young life.

Mid-afternoon, people began arriving in Pioneer Park under the big blue spruce trees Michelle had found so restful in the long, painful days of chemotherapy. Bright colored streamers fluttered in the breeze curling around pine branches and lacing from tree to tree. Multicolored balloons hung from the rustling boughs in swaying bunches like giant fruit.

A large, white, paper-covered board greeted guests with cheerful words of explanation: "Michelle thanks the City of Hope and all her many friends." The back of the board proudly held mementos of the past 18 months—letters from the White House, newspaper articles about Michelle and the family, her two silver skiing medals and pictures of her skiing, letters from Senator Edward Kennedy, a letter from Totie Fields, a photograph of Wayne Newton and other things of importance to Michelle.

Before long, nurses, technicians, family friends, people from the church, therapists, and others were milling around under the trees.

"Where's Michelle?" Linda asked Laura.

"I don't really know," she said a little puzzled. "She wanted to come on her own. Kimmy went to find her a few minutes ago."

"It looks like some of these folks are on coffee breaks," Linda said looking around at the many uniformed people standing nearby.

"I know," Laura said putting the cake knife down on the table. "I'm going to see what's taking so long."

As Laura moved toward the children's wing the side door opened and Michelle in a wheelchair, Kaylene, Billie and a half dozen more children with assorted medical paraphernalia came toward her, smiling happily. Dressed in party garb, bathrobes and pajamas they made their way toward the trees.

"What took so long, honey?" Laura asked gently, feeling the pressure of people waiting for them to get things started.

"I had to wait for my friends," she said looking back over her shoulder and smiling. "Some of them move kinda slow." Laura looked at the children making their way toward the trees. Little Billie walking just ahead of Michelle's wheelchair, his blue and yellow striped T-shirt pulled across a bulging abdominal tumor, inoperable. Lisa, wearing a head scarf over her sparse and scraggly hair, white tape holding an arm board to her left arm protecting the IV shunt still in her veins. Kaylene, smiling now as she shyly surveyed the festive scene ahead of them, bravely fighting her battle against a brain tumor.

Michelle knew how important a day like today would be to these friends. It's important to share good times; time is so short. What made today special for Michelle was sharing it with others who shared in the same kind of pain. Time to smile is important to those who see how fragile life really is.

Sitting quietly on a folding chair under a weathered old evergreen, Joy Sutera watched the little procession of hospital patients collecting under the trees. Michelle happily checked on her friends like a mother hen, laughing, teasing, making them feel at ease. Joy smiled to herself as she watched the little girl, thinking, *Michelle really enjoys showing love, gets lost in others so easily.*

She glanced at the hem of Michelle's skirt, to the one leg sticking out in front. A runner she had seen that morning came back into her mind and she reviewed the easy, rhythmic movement of his two strong legs as he jogged along the street. The powerful muscles of his thighs, the taut calves straining to meet his demands to push on further, to bear the weight, to move him smoothly along the road. She had watched the man, working his way along the pavement away from her as she pondered the question building inside, "Why, God? Where's the justice? How can anyone face what Michelle has to face?"

She focused on Michelle chattering happily with her friends. Joy's trained nurse's eye saw other things under the cheerfulness Michelle projected so easily. She knew the child's face was thinner, her eyes darker and deeper than usual. Chemotherapy always makes them lose weight; they are so sick for days. Her hair was scraggly and sparse, hardly grown back since the last treatment.

But her spirit! That was radiant. So many of the children she'd seen just seemed to lose their spark. The days and weeks of illness and limitations placed on them so often beat them down, robbing them of their color and personality.

Michelle's spirit soared, her peace and confidence showing through all the outward reminders of the ravages of her illness and the toll it took on her daily. She was a real and challenging encouragement to others. She was living proof of God's gentle care and strong protection in time of greatest need.

That's it, isn't it, Lord? Joy thought silently. *Michelle offers hope. What you've done for her is keep your promise. Anyone who trusts you and takes you at your word can know the same peace. Her peace is so real. Her trust and her dependence on you are strong and genuine—and—it's mine too. I understand that now.*

"Oh, God," Joy whispered as she walked toward Michelle, "thank you."

"Gray elephant!" Michelle chirped. "Stop, Kim!! Let me out of this thing!" She grabbed her crutch from beside her in the wheelchair and bounded toward Joy, using the crutch like a spring. She surrounded Joy with a hearty hug and enormous grin. "You came! I'm so glad!" she whispered.

"So am I," Joy said hugging the little girl tightly. The words came from the depths of her heart.

Soon Michelle was ceremoniously cutting the cake and passing it around. The punch was served and Michelle smiled happily as she looked around at her friends, family, young and old, enjoying her party. Joyce Klein was there; people from the church were enjoying themselves; friends from the neighborhood came; Linda Kurz, Joy, favorites from x-ray and the labs, nurses, Dr. Rosen, Dr. Kramer and others who had touched her life in some way.

As they talked over their cake, Michelle glanced toward a tall man in tan slacks and a short-sleeved shirt strolling toward her. She dropped her cake plate to the ground beside her metal folding chair and, steadying herself on her friend Nikki's shoulder, stood up. Sure now that she recognized the man she loped toward him. He grinned as she called out, "Dr. Moor! You came to my party."

With unbridled enthusiasm she flung her crutch off to the side and hopped the last few feet with her arms open wide. He reached out to catch her as she threw both arms around his middle, hanging on tightly. "I'm so glad to see you," she said breathlessly.

"And I'm glad to see you too," Dr. Moor said sincerely. "If you weren't such a famous TV star I probably wouldn't have heard about your party."

"You heard on TV?" she looked up with wonder.

Laura reached them and warmly welcomed the surgeon. "We're so glad you came," she said, "we tried to reach you but no one here knows your latest address."

"Well, it's funny how I heard about it," he said as they began walking toward the cake table, "I had been reading quite late one night last week and decided to take a little break, so I turned the TV on for a few minutes, and there was Michelle. I couldn't believe my eyes."

"Were you surprised?" Michelle asked hopefully.

"I'll say I was," he answered. "I hadn't heard anything at all about the award. It was wonderful to see that happen after all she's been through," he added sincerely to Laura. "Then you mentioned the party today and I thought I'd just drop by and see what I could see."

Michelle hugged him around the waist again, "I'm so glad you came. I've missed you so much. I was afraid you would forget me."

"Forget you?" he said smiling. "Let me show you something I brought along. Remember the little letter you wrote me when I left here?"

"Sure. I drew pictures on it, too."

He pulled the paper off a small package he'd brought with him, and held up a picture frame for Michelle to see. Under the glass was her letter to Dr. Moor.

"This hangs on the wall just above my desk, Michelle, and every day I remember a very sweet young lady I met at the City of Hope when I was here."

Michelle looked at the letter and then up at Dr. Moor. Her eyes spoke the thank yous her heart felt but couldn't put into words, and the doctor immediately forgot the long, hot drive to the little girl's party.

The air was filled with the sweet song of birds as they flew from tree to tree above the party. The breeze pushed balloons around and the children laughed, enjoying a longed-for break in their hospital routine. Michelle's party was a success. There was just one thing left to do.

With great ceremony Michelle pulled a lovely wooden plaque from its hiding place and approached Dr. Rosen who stood in the shade near the table holding his glasses in his hand. The two lines between his eyebrows deepened as he puzzled over what was happening.

Then Michelle briefly explained that she and her family appreciated so much the care they'd received at the City of Hope that they wanted to present them with a special thank you. He smiled warmly and read each word on the plaque.

"Well," he said still smiling, "you're not the only one who gets to make a presentation today, Michelle." He reached into the front of his lab coat and pulled out a white slip, handed it to Dick and said, "It's Michelle's tomography report. After 18 months her lungs are still clear. There are no signs of any new problems."

Dick and Laura read the report and hugged each other and the doctor. Today was indeed a day for celebration. They'd given her less than four percent chance of survival over a year ago, and God was ignoring their predictions. No man can limit God.

As Dr. Rosen excused himself to return to his duties, he asked Laura, "Would you be willing to speak to our psychological committee next Wednesday morning?"

"What kind of a committee is that?" she asked. "What could *I* tell *them*?"

"It's a group of doctors, psychologists, occupational therapists and other interested professionals. We meet once a month to discuss methods of improving our treatment of the children here, and one area of interest is patient acceptance with catastrophic disease. Michelle was so well prepared and has accepted what has happened to her so positively we'd like to ask you some questions about how you've handled this as a family."

Laura looked at Dick, then back at the doctor. "I'd like to talk to these people as long as I can say what I want to say."

"They will listen, Mrs. Price," Dr. Rosen assured her, nodding his head. "Our purpose is to help others adjust the way Michelle has. There are things you've done as a family we'd like to teach other families to do. We want to know what those things are. No one will challenge what you say."

"Then I'd love to come."

Wednesday morning came and, before long, Laura walked through the door with Dr. Rosen into a small room near the nurse's station. Seated in scattered chairs were seven or eight men and women, most wearing white lab coats. They continued talking quietly among themselves until Dr. Rosen called them to order.

"By way of introduction, I'd like you to meet Mrs. Laura Price," he said gesturing toward Laura. Then opening a large file on his lap he continued, "She and Mr. Price brought their daughter, Michelle, eight years old, to us in . . ." He scanned the sheet in front of him, "November of 1976. She presented with a history of tenderness in the right tibia. Pain was severe, though intermittent, beginning 10 to 12 weeks prior to admission. She saw her family physician who ordered a series of x-rays done which showed suspicion of a tumor. She was subsequently admitted to Children's Hospital where they did a biopsy, and the biopsy showed *osteogenic sarcoma*. The parents requested another opinion and the child was transferred to the City of Hope, where amputation of the right leg above the knee was performed." He closed the chart and laid it in his lap.

"The Prices have done a magnificent job of preparing their daughter for surgery," he continued. "The child faced the reality of what was happening to her before surgery ever took place. Since her adjustment was so smooth and unusual, I have invited Mrs. Price to share with us what she can about what they as a family have done to help their daughter adjust so smoothly and so completely."

Laura swallowed hard as Dr. Rosen turned the floor over to her. She whispered a prayer that God would do the speaking and then she opened her mouth.

"I appreciate the chance to speak to you today, and I hope something I say might help other children in Michelle's position some day. We've been so pleased with the treatment here. It means a lot to us that you care so much.

"First of all, I want you to know that what Dick and I did to help our daughter understand what was happening to her couldn't really be considered unusual. We're not super parents, just simple people with a strong belief in God, and we're not strangers to hard times at our house. Just six months before we found out about Michelle's tumor, our 20-year-old son was run over on the freeway by a semi-truck, and left for dead. The doctors said he could not live, but we kept praying and watched God restore Rick to complete health. Michelle shared in every day of that experience with us and saw God provide for her brother's serious physical needs. She knew He wouldn't let her down. We all share the belief that God cares for each one of us personally.

"That's the basis of our accepting things that take place in our life, as individuals and as a family. We all believe that nothing touches our life that hasn't first passed through the hands of our heavenly Father. Nothing."

Laura looked around the room and was almost surprised at the attentive expressions on the faces looking back at her as she spoke.

"We have always made it a family practice," Laura continued, "to cry *together* when somebody is hurting. That's why one of us stayed here in the hospital with Michelle the whole time. We hurt together, and there's a great deal of strength when you know your hard times are shared by those you love."

The doctors and others in the room asked Laura questions about specific ways she and Dick handled things, for instance, how they told Michelle she would lose her leg. They asked about how they comforted her during chemotherapy, and other common areas the other patients face. Laura answered their questions as completely as she could, reminding them, "When you believe God has a purpose it's easier to accept what comes."

When the meeting was over and people were leaving the room, one woman stopped Laura and said coldly, "You know, no one here believes the way you do, but we've found that people with your kind of faith are the ones who handle these things so well."

Laura looked into the woman's eyes and calmly said, "I was asked to share what we've done with Michelle. That's all I did. I can't do anything at all about what you choose to believe. You have to decide for yourself."

"Well," she said under her breath as she walked through the door, "I don't believe it for a minute."

Lord, Laura prayed silently as she drove along the freeway later, *those educated, intelligent people heard your word today and you promised your word wouldn't return void. Press it firmly into their hearts and use it to touch even one life for you.*

13
Beginning Again

"You gonna wear your wig?" Laura asked Michelle as they scurried around, getting ready for the City of Hope luncheon. In all their 65 years these supporters of the City of Hope had never invited a patient or a family to share their experiences with them. This year they'd made an exception.

"It's itchy," Michelle called back from her room. "It makes my head scratchy, and I feel weird with hair."

Laura looked over her shoulder at Dick and shrugged. "You'd think she could stand it for a few hours for something like this," she said shaking her head.

"Well, honey," he said squinting at a knotted shoelace, "if you think she should wear it why don't you tell her so?"

"No," she said thoughtfully securing a thin strand of beads around her neck. "That's like telling her she's not good enough the way she is. If it doesn't bother her to be bald it sure shouldn't bother me to look at her."

Michelle bounded into the room and backed up to Laura, "Zip my dress, Mommy," she said. "Can I wear my new horse necklace? I'll take good care of it I promise."

"Sure," Laura said pulling on the zipper. "It would look real nice on this." She put both hands on Michelle's shoulders, turned her around and looked at her for a long moment, then pulled her close and hugged her. "We sure love you."

"I love you guys too," Michelle responded brightly.

"I don't know why you want to love the likes of her," Dick teased finally working his shoestring loose. "Price, you're basically no darn good."

Michelle looked at her father out of the corner of her eye, then moved slowly toward him, slipping her arm around his shoulder coyly. "But, Daddy," she protested in a southern drawl, "ah'm *exactly* like you."

"Well, in that case," he said laughing, "I guess you're not so bad after all."

The International Ballroom at the Beverly Hilton Hotel was crowded and buzzing on the hot July afternoon. The luncheon today marked the finish of a weekend conference for the supporters of the City of Hope. Many of those in attendance were among the wealthiest, most influential people in all of California. Everywhere were people in fine clothing in tasteful, classic style. The air was alive with excitement.

The Prices were seated at a round table to the right of the room with easy access to the stage. Dazzling white tablecloths, laid with fine silver settings and lovely china surrounded a centerpiece of pastel carnations and greenery.

Michelle sat beside her mother, taking everything in. "Mom," she asked under her breath, "how come they give you so many forks?"

Laura patiently explained what the forks were for and smiled slightly as she answered Michelle's many other questions that came before the meal.

"Do they have a ladies' room?" Michelle asked.

"I'll show you where it is," volunteered Mrs. Nelson, a finely dressed lady sitting at the table. "I'm just on my way there myself," she added extending her hand and a smile to Michelle as she pushed her chair back and stood up.

They walked together through the double doors a few feet behind the table and were gone only a few minutes when Kim poked Laura and hoarsely whispered, "Look!"

Laura turned around, her mouth dropping open at what she saw. Just inside the double doors, out of the full view of other eyes, stood Michelle. Her head scarf was gone and in its place sat Mrs. Nelson's reddish pompador wig. Kim giggled and Laura covered her eyes with her hand, shaking her head as Michelle turned slowly in the doorway for full appreciation. Pleased with the results, she flashed an impish grin at her mother and sister and disappeared.

"What's Mrs. Nelson doing in the ladies' room all this time without her wig?" Kim said giggling.

"Poor thing," Laura gasped, regaining her composure, "I wonder whose idea that was?" The flush of her cheeks was becoming to her.

Before long Mrs. Nelson and Michelle made their way back to the table. Michelle's head scarf was tied neatly around her head, and Mrs. Nelson didn't have a hair out of place. No one said a word as they began seriously eating their fruit salad.

After the meal and a short introduction the Prices stepped to the microphone. Michelle waited at the table. Trembling, Laura laid her papers on the podium and began to speak.

"I hope you'll excuse me," she said breathlessly, "I'm very nervous." Then, holding her papers tightly in both hands she began, "June sixteenth there was a very special party held under the trees next to the rose garden at the City of Hope. The trees were in bloom with streamers and balloons. There was pink punch and a cake, decorated with a rose garden and waterfall, served by friends. It wasn't a birthday and it wasn't a holiday. It was Chemo-Completion Day!

"There was a large sign: 'Michelle thanks the City of Hope and all her many friends.'

"Chemo-Completion Day marked the end of 18 long months of treatment for Michelle, our daughter. It was a day that she had planned and talked about for months. She wanted to share a special day with the many people who had cared for and visited her, and she wanted to thank God for the strength and inner peace He gave her through it all. Michelle's faith has remained strong and constant.

"The rose garden has a very special meaning for Michelle. It was there that her father and I told her about the malignant tumor in her leg. When we asked Michelle why she picked the rose garden for her party she couldn't put it in words, only that it's special to her and one of her favorite places.

"It must be obvious by the very fact that Michelle wanted to give a party for everyone at the City of Hope that they have indeed become a very special part of our hearts and lives."

She folded her papers in half and leaned a little closer to the microphone to add, "We do love you all and appreciate you for making the City of Hope possible.

"Now I'd like to introduce our daughter, Kim."

Kim stepped to the podium. "As Michelle's sister I'd like to thank you too, and I'd like to read a poem to you that was written for Michelle by a family friend, Ken Millett. It kind of expresses what I feel about my little sister:

> Michelle is in God's ministry
> Proof He really cares,
> Evidence His love exists
> To answer all our prayers.
> She's smiling but it's painful,
> Courage demands a toll.
> Her strength is somewhere deeper
> In the unseen, living soul.
> The courage Michelle gives others
> By using her one leg well,
> Proves Victors aren't impossible.
> She stands where once she fell.

The audience was visibly moved by what had been said so far. Here and there around the room handkerchiefs were appearing.

"Laurie mentioned she was nervous," Dick began as he stepped to the mike. "I'm so nervous I was thinking maybe I'd duck out the back door and send a telegram."

The audience laughed, grateful for a light spot to rest momentarily, but still eager to hear more.

"May 20, 1976 is another date we will remember," Dick continued. "Our son, 20-year-old Rick, was run over by a semi-truck on the freeway." Dick's voice began to thicken, "Every wheel . . ." He paused to regain his composure. "Every wheel on the left side of the truck", he choked on the words, "and trailers passed over Rick's body. He wasn't expected to live. But God intervened and Rick is alive and well today."

Tears glistened in Dick's eyes and the thickness in his throat stopped the words again. He cleared his throat and explained haltingly, "I still relive that once in awhile."

Regaining control he continued, "This experience taught us the importance of faith and a day-by-day relationship with God. Six months later, to the day, we were to draw on that faith again. We learned that our daughter, Michelle, had a malignant bone tumor and was going to lose a leg. Michelle was in a large hospital when we learned the gravity and the nature of the illness. We sought second opinions and were directed to the City of Hope.

"After a warm reception and a complete tour of the facility, we sat down with the doctor and were informed of the philosophy, treatment and prognosis.

"We were greatly impressed with the concept that the family plays an important role in the recovery and well-being of the patient. We at no time were shunted to a remote waiting room and left to wonder what was going on. The consideration shown our family will always be remembered and appreciated. . . ." His voice faded off again as tears pressed against his throat momentarily.

"At the City of Hope the focus is on the recovery of the patient. Money has never distracted family or patient from this goal. This in itself is therapeutic. During this time we learned the meaning of the word *sadaka* —righteous giving.

"We welcome this opportunity as a family to personally thank all of you, and I'm sure these sentiments are shared by all the other families and patients. Thank you."

Dick reached into the pocket of his suit and pulled out a small parcel of blue papers. "Before introducing Michelle I would like to read a letter she received from her cousin. It's another episode from the rose garden which is sort of a focal point for us, a beautiful place where we have shared many good and many tragic times.

" 'Michelle: Remember our games in the rose garden? Isn't it strange that among all the roses we saw, we only wanted to pick maybe one or two? Why did we pick the most beautiful rose that could be found in the whole garden? I don't think we wanted to hurt the rose or punish it for being beautiful. We just wanted to take it to a place where we could show it off. To a place where it could bring more joy to more people. Now all the people who come to visit you who don't have time to take a walk in the rose garden will be able to share its beauty with you.

" 'Remember the other rose in the garden that was so beautiful you wanted to pick just one petal from it? That was a special rose, too. And when it blossoms it will be big and strong and beautiful and different from all the other roses, because, as you and I know, it will have one less petal than the rest.' "

Dick swallowed hard at the lump that would not let him speak, and tears flowed down his cheeks as he finished the last paragraph, " 'Michelle, to me all people are like roses and you are a very special rose who has brought joy and strength to the world around us. You are among the rest of us, the most beautiful rosebud in the rose garden and I love you very much. Your cousin, Jim.' "

Clearing his throat one last time he said, "In the last few months we have heard our daughter referred to in many ways: Miss Wonderful, a powerhouse, cheerful, uncomplaining, funny, special, an incredible young lady. Now here she is, our special rose—Michelle."

As though on cue the audience stood to its feet smiling through tear-filled eyes, applauding as Michelle made her way across the long stage to the podium. She smiled widely as she looked intently into the faces of her family. Each member as valued as the whole, each one caring for the others, together, strengthened because of the unseen member, Christ, the giver of the love they shared.

As the applause died down, people took their seats again, and Michelle said in a clear voice, "I just want to thank you."

Then amid resounding applause the family took their seats at the table once again. The main speaker followed them to the podium and looked quietly after them until they were settled at the table.

"You know," he said intimately into the mike, "maybe we need to change the saying to 'I *did* promise you a rose garden.' "

People sought out Michelle and the family after the luncheon to thank them for coming, to tell how they had been touched. Many shared their own experiences, miracles they'd seen in their own lives.

In the car on the way home as everyone chattered about what people had said, Dick listened quietly for several miles, struggling with his feelings.

God, he prayed silently as they sped along the road, *I'm even ashamed to admit this to you, but I'm—jealous, actually jealous of* other people's miracles. He thought back over the words and sorted through his feelings a little more.

It's like, when I hear about something you've done in someone else's life I compare it with what you've done for us. Like a little kid at Christmas, sizing up everybody else's presents to make sure his were the biggest and best.

That's awful! he thought, genuinely unhappy with what his honesty was revealing in the private corners of his life.

It's wonderful basking in the warmth and comfort of our miracles—Rick and Michelle. I love sharing what you've done for us. Others are so encouraged, so thrilled by your powerful intervention in their lives.

The trouble is I've almost forgotten what it's like to live without being special to other people because of what you've done. He wondered as he drove on, *Why do you perform miracles, Lord?*

You've opened doors for us to tell people about you. That's got to be a part of it. But we've also learned firsthand about how you can work in a person's life.

Thoughts darted through his mind as he pondered this new truth, *Miracles are sent for growth then, a point that requires some kind of action; a place where we can regroup and change directions in our lives. If we just keep looking for miracles we miss the touch of reality, we forget to go where the work waits to be done.* He smiled slightly to himself, *Jealous of someone else's miracles. Thank you, Lord, for growing me a little more today. Help me to encourage others and to share in the joy of miracles you perform in their lives. And thanks for not being small and shortsighted like I am. What a mess this old world would be in if you left me in charge of things. Just keep teaching me, Lord. And be patient. I'm a slow learner.*

The warm weather continued and Laura packed a large sack with goodies. Michelle and a couple of friends piled into the car and they headed for the beach. The sun was warm early and it promised to be a beautiful day. The girls chattered happily all the way to the coast and galloped like young colts across the long stretch of sandy beach to a spot they chose beside the water's edge. Michelle sank her crutch into the sand again and again as she bobbed along keeping stride with the others.

Blankets stretched across the warm sand, Laura suddenly found herself buried under shorts and T-shirts as the girls pulled them off and flung them back toward the blanket on a dead run to the water.

"Last one in the water's a rotten egg," Michelle hollered pushing her crutch into the sand and heading toward the breakers.

"You're gonna be the rotten egg," Cara called back over her shoulder as she raced past Michelle onto the cold, wet sand.

"Oh, yeah!" Michelle said, delight and determination flashing in her eyes as she dropped her crutch and hopped, neck and neck with both friends the rest of the way up to their waists into the Pacific.

Squeals of delight and ripples of giggles harmonized with the sound of crashing waves and calling gulls. Laura smiled from her dry perch on the blanket and watched the girls wrestling and splashing along the edge of the water. She turned, collecting the clothes lying around the blanket, and glanced at the couple beside her.

"Look at that little kid," the young woman was saying to her companion. "She's missing a leg and she's as bald as a cue ball."

"That's gross," he responded. "They shouldn't let kids like that on a public beach."

Laura couldn't believe she was hearing what she knew she heard. She sat there in silence watching these two strangers discuss Michelle like a piece of meat. She wanted to stand up and scream, "How dare you even think things like that about that child. After what she's been through, after the battles she's fought just to stay alive, after the love she's shown to others . . . how dare you!" She wanted to tell them how wrong they were.

She looked back at the ocean and Michelle holding tightly to Cara's arm on one side, Debbie on the other. The three of them worked their way into the breakers and body surfed back to shore laughing and tumbling in the salty water. There was just no way to hide a missing leg when you're wearing a two-piece bathing suit.

Hide? Is that what I want to do? Laura searched her feelings just now. *It is what I'd do if I could. I'd hide her so nobody could hurt her with what they think or say. And I'm the one who wanted her to wear a wig. How fickle feelings are.*

She turned over and lay down on the blanket. It felt warm under her as she reached into the sand and pushed a few tiny grains around with her fingernail. Dropping her hand into the warm sand she pushed against it moving her fingers back and forth until her entire hand was buried under the soft grains. She looked at her arm and realized that it looked as though she had no hand. For several minutes she studied her arm and tried to imagine what it would be like to lose a limb.

God, she prayed silently, *don't ever let me forget these people's faces and somehow teach me to reach out to them in their fear. Help me to make them understand, to help them accept people like Shelly—just the way they are.*

The day was an exhausting success and mid-afternoon they headed home, sandy and sunburned. Michelle pulled the CB mike from its cradle, pressing the button on the side.

"Breaker, breaker, this is Bald Eagle. Anybody got their ears on out there? Come in, good buddy."

The girls laughed as a trucker called "Bushwhacker" responded to her call as they sped toward home. Laura smiled at Michelle's chosen handle, Bald Eagle. *Lord, just let me accept things the way she does.*

14
A Single Step

"OK, Michelle," the physical therapist said as she set the package on the floor. "Here it is."

"My leg?" she asked with anticipation.

"That's right, your new leg." Nancy opened the top of the package and reached inside with both hands pulling the artificial leg out and standing it on the floor where Michelle could get a good look at it. It was already wearing a sock and Michelle's matching shoe.

Her eyes opened wide as she looked the prosthesis up and down. "It looks like a doll leg, Nancy," she commented.

"Want to try it on?"

"I guess so," she answered a little hesitantly. She watched Nancy and did what she was told, and before long she was standing with her stump inside the socket of the artificial limb.

"Now," Nancy continued, "take that strap and wrap it around your waist. . . ."

"Like this?" Michelle asked, pulling it around her left hip.

"Exactly. You're a quick learner," she smiled at her small patient. "Now, hook the strap here and let's get a look at you."

As the therapist backed away a couple of steps for a better look, Michelle caught sight of her own image in the wall of mirrors. She studied what she saw for several seconds. "Maybe with pants on it won't look so ugly," she said, then turned to face her mother. "Well," she said smiling proudly, "what do you think?"

"I think you've gotten taller in the last few months and I didn't notice," Laura said over the lump in her throat. "You look great, honey."

"Well, good," the therapist said smiling. "Now all we have to do is get you to work this thing right and we're on our way. We've got some work to do here, Michelle."

Laura closed the door behind her and breathed a sigh of relief as she walked down the hall into the sunlight. It was so bright it took her a few seconds to adjust, but she welcomed the warmth falling across her shoulders. The sky was clear and blue and there was a light breeze playing in the trees nearby. She settled onto the sweet smelling grass and filled her lungs with the fresh air of another new day.

"Thanks, Lord," she whispered. She hadn't been looking forward to this morning. She'd been concerned that this new leg might be as traumatic for Michelle as the first had been. *That first leg—I'll never forget the look in her eyes when she saw that thing,* Laura thought, *and I didn't blame her. The screws all exposed, leather parts showing—it looked like something an old sailor would have carved for himself at sea.*

It's funny, she reflected, *until I saw Michelle with an artificial leg I didn't realize how natural it had become for her to have only one. But with the prosthesis standing in the corner or flung across her bed it's a constant reminder of the loss.* She straightened her legs out in front of her and leaned back on both arms, turning her face up into the sun. For a few minutes she just concentrated on the warmth, then she opened her eyes and looked into the endless blue sky. "Lord," she said quietly, "keep us from weakening under the daily-ness of all this. Keep us strong, and close to you."

After weeks of practice, the day came when Michelle rode proudly home with her leg on the seat between her and Kim.

"Let's go by and show Jim," she suggested enthusiastically, and before long Laura pulled the car up at the curb in front of their cousin's house.

"Jim," Michelle yelled excitedly bursting through the door of his apartment, "I got it! I got my leg today. Want to see?"

"Of course I want to see," Jim said grinning. "I can't wait. Go put it on."

She felt like all thumbs trying to get into her leg in her excitement. Always before there was someone to help her with it, but this time she wanted to do it all alone. She finally worked the leg into position, snapped the belt around her waist and stood up beside the bed. Her balance was good and she walked through the door smiling to herself.

"Well," she said as she neared the top of the stairway, "what do you think?" Jim and Laura turned to see her smiling broadly down at them.

"Look at you," Kim said walking up behind her on the landing, "you've got two legs." She hugged her little sister tightly. "Well, show us how it works," Kim added.

"I'm coming downstairs," Michelle announced moving to the top step.

Laura started slowly up the stairs toward Michelle, "Honey," she said, "why don't you start with something a little easier?"

"I can do it, Mom," she said clearly disappointed in Laura's cautiousness. "I'm not a cripple."

She took hold of the railing with both hands and started slowly, carefully down the short stairway. Each step was another victory for the little baldheaded girl with the leg like a doll, and as she mastered one step after another she smiled to herself.

Halfway down Jim reached out and touched her hand, his eyes filled with pride.

"How about that, Jim?" Michelle said. "Now I won't have to use crutches."

"It's wonderful, Michelle," he said. "I knew you could do it. Pretty soon you'll be as fast as you are with your crutches."

She just grinned up at him as she stepped onto the carpet at the bottom of the stair. "And now I can wear two shoes again."

She did a few soft shoe steps and then worked her way back up the stairs to take the leg off. Stopping at the top she leaned on the railing. "Mom," she said with a flash of genius, "I just had a great idea!"

"What's that?" Laura asked.

"Remember Matt, the kid at school who used to kick me in the leg all the time?"

"Uh-huh."

"Well," she said hunching up her shoulders and rubbing her hands together like a mad scientist, "I'm going to wear my leg back to school some day and I won't tell him it's fake, see, and I won't snap it on tight. So when he kicks me again, my leg will fly right out of my pant leg and clear across the playground. That'll cure him of kicking anybody ever again," she said triumphant in the thought of such a beautiful plan of revenge.

Later that night as Dick and Laura settled into bed Laura lay staring up at the dark ceiling for several minutes. "Billy died last week," she said quietly.

The words hung in the darkened room. "Oh no," Dick whispered, grateful the darkness hid his tears. "He fought so hard for life."

"You know," Laura said quietly, "I think medicine is a lot like Christianity."

"What do you mean, honey?" Dick asked.

"Well," she said slowly, resting her head against his shoulder thinking it out, "a nurse can give two patients good care and the right medication, and one lives and the other dies."

"Yeah," he said grasping the parallel, "and a Christian can pray for two people, love them as God would, do everything 'right,' and one becomes a child of God and the other goes his way without Christ."

"There isn't any way to tell who will make the choice and who won't."

"You have to give your best to all of them, and let them make the final choice themselves," Dick said.

They moved closer together, into each other's arms and Laura whispered, "I'm so sorry about Billy. I know Billy's with Jesus, but I'm so sorry it ended for him so early. How lonely his parents must be tonight."

Several months later, through an article in a large magazine, Tom Clark of the Arabian Horse Association learned about Michelle's gift from Wayne Newton and extended an invitation to the Prices for Michelle to participate in the 1981 Arabian Horse Pentathlon in Oklahoma City, Oklahoma. It was exciting, and an opportunity for Michelle to develop her riding ability in preparation for the event. But several people involved were concerned about using Prince.

"Honey, you have to try to understand," Laura reasoned with Michelle. "Prince is nearly 11 years old. To try to train him now to do the things he'd have to do in the Pentathlon . . ." She shook her head slowly, "He's too old, Michelle. He won't live forever, honey. He's not a young horse anymore."

A few days later as Dick and Michelle drove home from the stables, she suddenly burst into tears.

"Shelly," he asked, "what's wrong?"

"Please, Daddy," she sobbed, "ask Mommy not to talk to me anymore about Prince getting older."

"But, we're all getting older, honey," he said as they pulled up at a stop light. He looked at her intently, "Mommy's getting older, and me too. Even you."

The light changed and shifting into first gear, Dick started across the intersection.

"But it doesn't bother me to think about you dying," she said.

He almost stalled the car, but managed to shift into the next gear before asking, "It doesn't bother you to think of us dying, but it does when you think about Prince dying? Thanks a lot, Price," he said half teasing.

"No, Daddy," she explained, "it doesn't bother me to think about you and Mommy dying because I know where you'll go when you die. But I don't know what will happen to Prince when he dies."

Dick drove silently for a few blocks. "Michelle," he said, "I don't know for sure either, but I'm sure we can trust God to do what's best. In the meantime, I'll talk to Mommy for you."

Looking out the window Michelle asked, "Daddy, do you know what I picture God like?"

"Tell me, Price."

"Well, I think He's a lover of all His animals. He'll be fun to be around, like He'll play hide-and-seek with me in the clouds when I get to heaven." She leaned back against the seat and thought a moment. Dick glanced at her out of the corner of his eye wishing he could see her full expression.

"I don't think He's like most kings who think they're hotshots and can't be with the regular people," she continued, reaching for her daddy's hand. "I think He'll be like one of us, but we'll really respect Him."

They rode in silence another mile or so, then Michelle patted Dick's hand and added, "You know, it's special the kind of love God has for us because He doesn't just pretend." She paused, watching the children on a playground. "He really loves us."

Dick glanced at the children running on the schoolyard and marveled at Michelle's consistent acceptance of God and life as they came to her.

"Daddy," she said as they pulled in the driveway, "I just want you to know, I'm not afraid to die."

Later that week Michelle called Laura into the bathroom where she was bathing. "Mommy," she said with fear in her eyes, "I think I felt some lumps under my arm."

Laura's blood ran cold at the words but she forced herself to check out the spot Michelle showed her. She felt several lumps on the inside of Michelle's right arm. They would have to be checked.

Sitting on the cold examination table the next afternoon Michelle studied the face of the young man checking her arm. She tried to read his eyes but couldn't penetrate the well-learned, noncommittal veneer. The silence in the room hung like heavy smoke as he slowly prodded and pushed, palpated and studied the small hard lumps under her skin.

Finally he straightened up, folding his arms across his chest. He looked hard at her shoulder from across the room, then raised his right hand to his chin, and slowly bit his lower lip. "Well," he said deliberately, "I don't think it's anything to worry about."

Michelle relaxed visibly at his words.

"We'll have Dr. Rosen take a look too, just to be thorough, but I'm sure it's just a couple of glands that have become irritated and infected from the crutches." He patted her knee, picking up the metal chart and tucking it under his arm. "You put your shirt back on now and I'll tell Dr. Rosen you're on your way over."

When the door closed behind the doctor, Laura unfolded Michelle's shirt and handed it to her. She looked into her daughter's eyes and asked, "Were you scared, honey?"

"Worse than that," she answered pulling her T-shirt over her head and letting out a deep sigh, "I was terrified!"

"Were you afraid it might be cancer again?" Laura asked, moving beside Michelle and smoothing down the short brown hair that was coming slowly back.

"Yeah, but that part doesn't scare me so much." She studied her hands in her lap. "It's the treatments," she said quietly. Then raising her eyes to meet her mother's, she softly added, "I don't think I could ever go through those treatments again."

Laura pulled her daughter close and held her for a moment. In 18 months of chemotherapy, Michelle had never once asked not to be taken for a treatment. She had never complained about the pain and violent sickness, or losing her hair; she was a model patient. God's grace was truly sufficient to her need.

She sat quietly beside her mother as they waited outside Dr. Rosen's office, tracing the pattern of the rug with her foot, sighing quietly.

"What're you thinking about?" Laura asked, softly touching Michelle's short brown hair.

"Just stuff," Michelle answered without looking up.

"Good stuff?" Laura continued, gently probing. "Or bad stuff?"

"Not really bad. . . ." Michelle pulled her leg into the chair, curling around to face her mother. "It's just . . ." she paused, thinking her words through, "it's just that, well, I'm afraid the boys aren't gonna like me." She searched her mother's kind eyes for reassurance or a little hope.

"You mean because of your leg?" Laura asked, trying to understand Michelle's real fears.

Michelle shifted in the chair, looking down at her fingers and nodded. Without looking up she added, "I try to look nice all the time. I comb my hair and I don't wear clothes with holes, and all that stuff, and I try to be friendly to everybody. But sometimes . . ." she paused thinking it through, "sometimes I think they just don't want a one-legged girl around." Tears filled her eyes as she looked to her mother for comfort.

Laura reached around Michelle and pulled her close. "Honey," she said gently, "I think only part of what you're feeling is because of your leg. A lot of it is just plain growing up. Sometimes that happens around your age.

"Almost-12-year-old girls feel kinda uncomfortable about boys, and boys feel the same way about the girls."

"Really?"

"Really," Laura assured her. "I remember thinking the boys didn't like me when I was your age, and I've got both legs."

Michelle thought about her mother's words, "But some of it *is* because of my leg, I know it is. At school there's lots of stuff I can't do now, at least not as good as I used to. So I get picked for a team just 'cause I'm the only one left and somebody *has* to pick me. They really don't want me on their side 'cause I can't help 'em win very much." Tears squeezed past her lashes and rolled down her face. "I don't blame 'em."

She rubbed her hand across her cheek abruptly wiping the tear away, wanting to wipe away the unfairness, suddenly angry that she hurt so much over something she could not control.

"I feel like quitting," she said, momentarily giving in to her frustration. "Even Maria picks Patty or Beth before me now. She used to say they couldn't play as good as I could." She looked off in space, remembering for a minute. "I miss my leg. Sometimes I really miss it."

As Michelle cried in her arms, Laura's thoughts drifted back to the day over three years before when this had all begun, the day she and Dick found out Michelle had a tumor.

The doctor had scheduled Michelle for a biopsy the morning after they'd found the tumor. On the way home from his office they'd stopped by the high school to get Kim.

Kim and her friends were practicing pom-pom drills on the football field when they found her and as soon as Michelle saw her sister she broke loose from Dick and Laura and ran down the green grassy slope, arms open, welcoming life inside. Kim turned and scooped Michelle up, whirling her round and round in circles. Their laughter echoed in the bleachers and poured across the deep pain that Dick and Laura bore.

Could it be possible that this would be the last time their little girl would run again? they had wondered that day. *Would the joy of being a child, of playing games and sharing with her friends be marred with tragedy? Would Michelle really be handicapped the rest of her life? How could this happen to a child? Their child?*

The questions were frightening and it had been far too soon for any of the answers, but fear lay like rocks at the bottoms of their stomachs in a dull ache. Dick stood behind the bleachers out of the girls' view, his shoulders heaving in great, deep sobs. Laura remembered now how he'd cried that day, as if his heart would break with its burden.

She looked at Michelle sitting beside her now. She was older, over three years older. She was tall and slender; a thick, lovely head of brown hair; deep, penetrating dark eyes; an infectious grin; and a faith that could move mountains. She was drawing on that faith again now, and today she struggled with an enemy Laura could not help her subdue, no matter how her mother heart ached to make things right for Michelle.

"I feel bad about feeling bad," Michelle said thoughtfully, interrupting Laura's thoughts. "God's gonna think I'm not grateful for what He's done. I think I'm looking at the bad too much, and not enough at what's good." She pondered her thoughts another minute, then added, "If I didn't have *any* arms or legs, I'd still have a mouth to praise God with."

"Now," Laura said smiling, "that's the Michelle I know and love." Then patting Michelle's hand gently she added, "Honey, no matter what happens, God isn't finished working His miracles in you. Nowhere near finished."

A Note from the Prices

When faced with the impending death of a loved one, fear and anxiety can be overwhelming. The message we hope will come through in this book is that regardless of the circumstances, God is *a very present help in time of trouble.* He does give *a peace that passes all understanding.*

We are ordinary people caught up in extraordinary circumstances. We live our ordinary lives through the grace of God. Our days are very similar to those of our friends and neighbors, though they face different lives, different struggles. Many people have said to us, "We don't know how you can do it. We don't think we could face what you've faced." Not only could you face our situation, but you could face it with peace and confidence—as long as you face it with God. He has already given us the solution to any problem; we only need to accept and act on His promises.

The lessons we've learned and continue to learn, all point to one thing—God means what He says. We only have to believe Him. In our situation—the near death of two of our three children—options were reduced to zero. God was the only alternative. That made the choice simple for us. The difficult part for us is applying this same principle—letting God do it *His* way—to our daily lives and receiving His help where we haven't exhausted all the alternatives. We're still growing!

We pray that you will be encouraged as you read, to place your faith and trust in God. He specializes in little problems and impossibilities. God has been the source of incredible joy in our lives—He loves *you,* and *cares* what happens in your life. That's what we hope we've shared with you in the pages of this book.

We would love to hear from you. Please write to us, Dick and Laura Price, c/o Regal Books P.O. Box 3875, Ventura, CA 93006.

Epilogue

Ending Michelle's story is the next best thing to impossible. She keeps meeting new challenges—*gold* medals in skiing, riding a float in the famed New Year's Day Rose Parade (1979), Grand Marshall in another, being asked to give the invocation at the Celebrity Equestrian Benefit, being part of the 1978 American Cancer Society success flier, and on and on. Collectible stories are endless—like the emergency room doctor's reaction when he heard that the little amputee had broken her hand rollerskating.

Michelle's story *has* no end. It will go on and on and as she is used of God she will encourage and challenge others with her faith.

One of Michelle's special friends, Ken Millett, has written a poem that says it all. It's called, "Perspective"

I suppose I'm supposed—
To keep winning in life,
With me, the "gold" is expected.
A little girl from the City of Hope
Whose courage the world respected.

I suppose I'm supposed—
To be impressed with myself,
For the way I coped with cancer.
But I'm really impressed with medicine
And with God for allowing the answer.

I suppose I'm supposed—
To be always first
In skiing the downhill race.
But victors sometimes are second—or last,
Despite the smile on their face.

I suppose I'm supposed—
To be humble and shy,
Instead of repeating my story.
But if telling about me gives others hope,
Then I give God the glory!